Your Guide to
Outstanding Early Childhood Practice in ICT

Hui-Yun Sung, John Siraj-Blatchford and Natalia Kucirkova

Contents

Published by Practical Pre-School Books, A Division of MA Education Ltd, St Jude's Church, Dulwich Road, Herne Hill, London, SE24 0PB.

Tel: 020 7738 5454 www.practicalpreschoolbooks.com

Associate Publisher: Angela Morano Shaw
Edited by: Rebecca Carey
Design: Alison Coombes **fonthill**creative 01722 717043

© MA Education Ltd 2016

ISBN 978-1-909280-77-9

Introduction

Raising expectations and achievement

This book was written in response to the new Information Communications and Technology (ICT) computing curriculum in the UK and in response to concerns about educational underachievement and especially, the underachievement of disadvantaged children.

According to the Organisation for Economic Co-operation and Development (OECD, 2014)[1], the gap between rich and poor is now at its highest level in 30 years in most OECD countries. At a global level, this gap has been amplified by the emergence of digital tools (Steyaert, 2002)[2], forming the so-called digital divides.

The negative effects of inequality may be considered the result of an underinvestment in education by people from disadvantaged social backgrounds (OECD, 2014)[1], or the result of the maximisation of educational investment opportunities by middle class parents (Ball et al., 1996[3]; Ball, 2003[4]). Heckman (2006)[5], a Nobel Prize-winner in economics, has shown that investments in early childhood programmes are justified by the returns provided to society as a whole. These issues are complicated, and at a global level, confounded by issues and concerns related to globalisation. In this book, these issues will be addressed directly on page 29. For now, it is enough to note that the importance of investments in the foundation stage of early childhood education has been widely highlighted in research, and has become a significant feature of public policy.

Institutions and governments around the world have an interest in addressing underachievement problems and helping bridge the social and digital divides between rural and urban disparities. International Aid agencies and charities have increasingly provided digital and non-digital technologies (e.g. books, toys, tablets, laptops and desktops) to rural communities and schools in middle and low income countries in order to bridge the rural-urban gaps. But in most global contexts, we have found that rural and disadvantaged children do not lack the technology so much as the adult support, effective pedagogies and motivations for learning. Indeed, the central issue regarding 'digital divides' does not reside in the divides between the 'have 'and the 'have nots' in terms of digital tools, but rather in terms of 'digital literacies'.

With the rapid evolution of ICT, increasingly young children own, access and use new technologies (e.g. handheld devices) on a daily basis. But while many parents value the importance of children's ICT skills for learning and future career, it is worth noting that not all content and information accessed through ICT is of educational value. The curricula and pedagogies that are relevant to ICT are crucial. Applied in the context of effective curriculum and pedagogy, ICT in early childhood should be recognised as providing a means to an end. It should be used as a tool to support and enrich children's learning.

Research has shown that mothers' qualification levels and family socio-economic status are strongly linked to children's learning outcomes. Conversely, research has also shown that it is what parents, teachers and other early childhood educators actively do that really matters. In particular, the Effective Provision of Pre-School Education (EPPE) project has revealed the importance of the home learning environment and parental involvement in activities for early childhood development and learning (Sylva et al., 2004)[6]. It has shown that many disadvantaged parents and pre-schools supporting disadvantaged communities provide effective support for children to achieve in education.

Substantial research is also now available providing evidence for the benefits of children using computers with adults' support and guidance. Working in a genuine partnership with disadvantaged parents and children, and equipping them with the necessary ICT knowledge and skills will empower them for education. The results could arguably be applied to children's use of handheld devices as well.

However, simply providing access to ICT is an ineffective way of addressing the gaps in skills and knowledge that exist in ICT usage. Therefore, the intention of this book is to offer guidance on how to effectively use ICT with young children. This book will be of value to people who work with young children, including parents, pre-school teachers, and library service providers.

The document mentioned overleaf (see Figure 1) demonstrates national standards for one of the 17 early years foundation stage profile early learning goals, and shows the level of learning and development expected at the end of the EYFS for technology. The main aim in achieving the goal is

summarised as follows "Children recognise that a range of technology is used in places such as homes and schools. They select and use technology for particular purposes." The document outlines that these skills include understanding the technology-related vocabulary (e.g. re-wind, fast forward), as well as knowing how to navigate a PC (e.g. scrolling down and selecting an image) and recognising the different functions of different devices (e.g. that a microwave can heat up things and a Bee-Bot® can be used to make up a maths game).

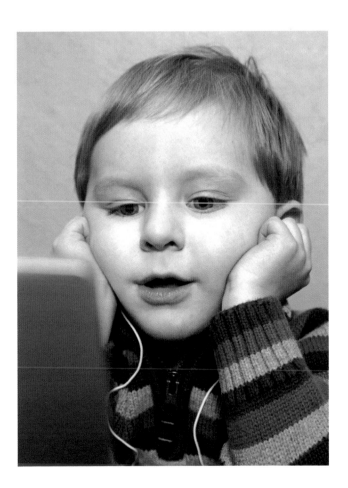

Figure 1

In September 2014, the UK introduced a coding curriculum which outlines that key Stage 1 pupils – that is 5-to-7 year olds – should be able to "understand what algorithms are, how they are implemented as programs on digital devices, and that programs execute by following precise and unambiguous instructions; create and debug simple programs and use logical reasoning to predict the behaviour of simple programs". Department for Education (2013). National Curriculum in England: Computing programmes of study (available at: https://www.gov.uk/government/publications/national-curriculum-in-england-computing-programmes-of-study/national-curriculum-in-england-computing-programmes-of-study).

Several organisations provide guidance on how to best implement these new requirements into existing teaching practice. For example, the UK Forum for Computing Education (http://ukforce.org.uk/) is an expert body, independent of government and awarding organisations, and their website is a comprehensive source of publications and other relevant resources for educators.

Clearly, different schools go about meeting these objectives in different ways. Most schools aim to embed these new objectives in all subject areas, as part and parcel of their everyday teaching practice rather than a separate subject or one-off activity. The levels of computing proficiency vary among individual children, however the new curriculum emphasises that all children can benefit from learning how to code, and encourages teachers to perceive it as a new way of thinking which can increase children's skillset.

An important guidance document on how to evaluate technology provision is the Early Learning Goal no15 focused on Technology (freely available from here: https://www.gov.uk/government/uploads/system/uploads/attachment_data/file/360542/ELG15__Technology.pdf).

References

1   The Organisation for Economic Co-operation and Development (OECD) (2014). Focus on inequality and growth–December 2014 (available at: www.oecd.org/social/inequality-and-poverty.htm).

2   Steyaert, J. (2002). Inequality and the digital divide: Myths and realities. In S. Hick, & J. McNutt (Eds.), *Advocacy, Activism and the Internet* (pp. 199–211). Chicago: Lyceum Press.

3   Ball, S., Bowe, R., & Gewirtz, S. (1996). School choice, social class and distinction: The realization of social advantage in education. *Journal of Education Policy*, 11(1), 89–112.

4   Ball, S. (2003). *Class Strategies and the Education Market: The Middle Classes and Social Advantage.* London: Routledge Falmer.

5   Heckman, J.J. (2006). Skill formation and the economics of investing in disadvantaged children. *Science*, 312(5782), 1900–1902.

6   Sylva, K., Melhuish, E.C., Sammons, P., Siraj, I., & Taggart, B. (2004). *The Effective Provision of Pre-School Education (EPPE) Project: Technical Paper 12–The Final Report: Effective Pre-School Education.* London: DfES/Institute of Education, University of London.

Literacy in early learning

One way of looking at differences among children and their early learning is in terms of vocabulary, that is, how many words a child has learnt in a given period. Research has shown that an average one-year-old uses about five words (Snow et al., 1998)[1]. But there are one-year-olds who do not speak, and other one-year-olds who have as many as thirty words in their vocabulary. This is an educational 'gap' that typically increases as children get older, so that at age two most children use about 150 words, but some only have ten and others have as many as 450 words. At age six we know that an average child in the USA or Europe knows as many as 14,000 words, but at this stage the vocabulary gap between children is enormous and extremely difficult to compensate for.

The most significant research explaining the causes of this gap dates from 1995, when a study by Hart and Risley (1995)[2]

found that professional parents spoke 72% more words to their children than working class parents. The children of professional parents also heard more than three times the number of words than children whose parents were receiving welfare benefits. They calculated that by the age of four, a typical child from a family receiving welfare benefits heard 32 million fewer words than a pre-school classmate from a professional family.

More recently, the Sutton Trust in the UK commissioned a series of vocabulary tests that were carried out by 12,500 British children at the age of five (Waldfogel & Washbrook, 2010)[3]. The study found that children from the poorest fifth of families were nearly a year behind children from middle income families in their results. They found that only 45% of the 20% poorest children ever had a bedtime story or have visited a library.[4]

The good news is that research has shown that high quality pre-school education can support children in catching up and succeeding, despite these early disadvantages. Following 400 hours of naturalistic observations of staff, and 254 systematic focal target child observations in pre-schools, the UK EPPE research projects (1997–2003, 2003–2012) found that the most effective pre-school settings provided both teacher-initiated group activities and freely chosen yet potentially instructive, play activities (Siraj-Blatchford et al., 2002)[5]. The research also identified "Sustained Shared Thinking" (SST) as a key feature of effective practice. This was defined as:

> *An episode in which two or more individuals "work together" in an intellectual way to solve a problem, clarify a concept, evaluate activities, extend a narrative etc. Both parties must contribute to the thinking and it must develop and extend (Siraj-Blatchford et al., 2002, p.8)[5].*

Subsequent research by Siraj-Blatchford (2007)[6] has extended the relevance of SST to show how effective adult-child 'shared activities' become progressively more sophisticated as the child develops their capability from the pre-verbal exchange of 'significant gestures', to 'improvised play', 'improvised collaboration' and 'more disciplined collaborations':

> *The development of these early (birth to age 6) 'Sustained Shared Thinking' activities (they all have this in common) are considered by many, and particularly by Russian neo-Vygotskian writers, to show a progression in learning activities[7] that are characterised by a transition from those focused upon "emotional communication with caregivers" (Lisina, 1986)[8], then to "object-centred joint activity" (Elkonin, 1989)[9] where the child begins object substitutions, and then on to Socio-dramatic play (Leontiev, 1964)[10], and finally activities that reflect the child's desire to learn more formally and embrace learning (or schooling) (van Oers 1999)[11] as the dominant learning activity (Siraj-Blatchford, 2007, p.16)[6].*

Gender equality in ICT

Globally, the reading opportunities provided through the growth in the use of mobile phones are of real significance for those marginalised groups in certain areas of the world, particularly for women and girls, and others who historically have not had access to paper books: "...research indicates that hundreds of thousands of people in countries like Nigeria, Ethiopia and Pakistan are reading full-length books on mobile phones, including phones with small, monochrome screens" (UNESCO, 2014)[12]. UNESCO also found that parents are increasingly using mobile devices to read to children to support their literacy acquisition and other forms of learning.

Around the world, women and girls appear to be as motivated as men to apply ICTs, and yet their access to the often relatively well-paid employment opportunities available in the ICT industries is quite limited. These problems are global, and the situation in the UK is only marginally worse than average for all the European Union (U15) nations, even though women's representation in the UK IT sector has declined in the past 10 years. In 2013 less than 16% of the 1,129,000 IT specialists in the UK were women. This lack of representation starts in secondary schools. While the girls opting for IT-related courses did consistently better than the boys, they only made up 44% of those enrolled in all related General Certificate of Secondary Education (GCSE) courses, and only 6.5% of those taking Computing A-level were girls. In higher education, girls accounted for just 18% of qualifiers from all Computer studies/ IT related courses. In the Computing and IT industry as a whole, women are equally well qualified as men but they are underrepresented, and earn 16% less (e-skills UK, 2014)[13].

In the past, the problem of the underrepresentation of women and girls in ICT has often been presented in terms of 'how can we provide a more accessible and motivating approach to ICT for girls'. In the UK, research carried out by the Office for Communication (OFCOM, 2013)[14] found that between the ages of 5 and 7, less than half the number of girls played computer or video games than boys, although they were twice as likely to use the Internet or to go online. This gap continues and widens into the teenage years. It seems that generally speaking, when it comes to IT use,

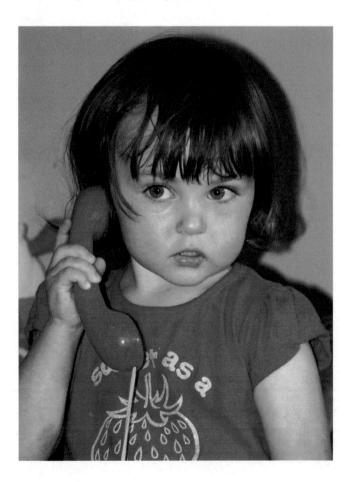

boys like computer games, whereas girls like to use IT to communicate. Siraj-Blatchford and Whitebread (2003)[15] refer to research carried out to identify so called 'pink software' games that would appeal more to girls. Laurel (1990)[16] found that girls enjoyed:

> ...*video game adventures where the leading characters are everyday people that they can relate to and where the major goal is to explore, with degrees of success and outcome. They also like games of discovery with strong 'realistic' story lines where success comes through collaboration and the development of friendships.*

However, some of the research suggests that even those girls who do play computer games tend to grow out of them, even if boys don't tend to (OFCOM, 2013)[14]. Computer games are also a very small sector within the overall IT industry, and the association of their early use with children's developing interest in the underlying technology has never been demonstrated.

Historically, the cultural expectations for (and of) girls in engineering and technology have undoubtedly been limited in most countries. However, in recent years, in response to demands from the industry for more skilled professionals, governments around the world have been making some efforts to encourage more women to enter the field through their educational policies, the setting up of awards and the provision of research funding.

Although cultural influences are deeply entrenched, it should be recognised that the fact that while many girls tend to be given dolls, and boys construction kits, the problem is more related to the comparative value given to these toys, and the commonly misleading assumptions being made about their relevance to computing and IT. Epstein (1995)[17] also refers to a study showing boys in early childhood explicitly using their gender to dominate construction activities. Boys' expectations are as relevant as those of girls in this respect. The teacher in Epstein's case study found it necessary to introduce 'girls only time' for the construction play to ensure equality of access. It is thus equally important to look carefully for any gender bias in access to ICT equipment in the classroom (Brooker & Siraj-Blatchford, 2002)[18].

Efforts have been made in many countries to remove gender stereotyped materials from schools and pre-schools, but many still remain. One example can be taken from a 1980s early reader for children in Taiwan. The text in Mandarin read: "Father gets up early to read newspapers" and "Mother gets up early to clean up [the house]". While in Taiwan and the UK, it was, until quite recent times, relatively common that mothers did all of the housework, many parents today do set a better example by sharing some of the house work. Women in many homes provide positive role models in programming domestic equipment such as washing machines, cooking equipment

and entertainment systems, and it is important to draw these competencies to children's attention.

One established way of countering historical stereotypes has been through the promotion of exemplar role models of women scientists and engineers. While women are seriously underrepresented, there are a few notable examples that have made it to the top such as Marissa Mayer, CEO at Yahoo. Jeannette Wing, the Corporate Vice President of Microsoft Research, could also be used as an inspirational role model for girls. Her example shows what can be achieved.

Wing is credited as being the first person to have coined the term 'Computational Thinking', and a new curriculum emphasis on computational thinking, rather than games may be just what is required to encourage more girls into IT. It is not just in our own experience that it has been found that girls are at least equally motivated and engaged in computing and IT as boys when they have been given the opportunity to develop their skills, in the context of developing their own practical priorities and computing and IT applications (Epstein, 1995[17]; Brooker & Siraj-Blatchford, 2002[18]):

> *This approach would...I suggest, serve to encourage girls to take up the subject, as girls tend to be more attracted to subjects that involve skills like collaboration and communication. I hesitate to engage in any kind of gender stereotyping, but in my experience what I've just said does tend to be true (Freedman, 2012)[19].*

Play and emergent literacy

Rogoff (2003)[20] and others have shown that a wide range of playful activities progressively engage children in the cultural life of adults and their communities around the world. Play provides the opportunity for children to consider objects abstractly. The wooden block, collection of Lego bricks, or other objects that the child plays with as a mobile telephone, become a means by which the meaning of 'real' mobile telephones can be explored through 'pretend'. The focus of the child's attention becomes: what is it that the object signifies, what can it do, what are its properties and functions – rather than its operation or representation in the 'real' world. The child is therefore able to explore the object in a more abstract and intellectual way. Programmable toys and on-screen programming and construction applications act in a similar way.

Both Vygotsky and Piaget saw play as a symbolic capacity building process. Play is fundamental to early learning and development, and it is essentially through play that children develop intellectually, creatively, physically, socially and emotionally in early childhood:

> The child moves forward essentially through play activity
> (Vygotsky, 1978, p.103)[21].

As Bodrova and Leong (2007)[22] suggested, early childhood educators can usefully intervene in children's play to improve its quality, but in doing so they should avoid being too directive and take care not to 'take over'. They can provide ideas, resources and props to stimulate and extend play.

Many of the computer programs that were first developed for young children provided 'drill and practice' in what many educators felt were the essential basic skills of literacy and numeracy. In practical terms, 'emergent literacy' is all about encouraging playful 'mark making' as a natural prelude to writing. It is about adults reading a range of different kinds of texts to children, and drawing their attention to the value and uses of text in the world around them.

Emergent approaches to literacy encourage 'literacy play' in the nursery; setting up pretend office play environments, libraries, and story books for children to integrate into their play. Educators who promote emergent literacy also provide positive role models by showing children the value that they place in their own use of print, and encourage the children to develop an emergent awareness of the nature and value of these resources for themselves.

Another thing that many educators committed to emergent literacy do, is to encourage parents to read to their children and ensure that the children see them reading for their own purposes. In fact, large-scale research projects looking at the development of early literacy have shown the significant value of parents reading to children and taking them to the library (Hannon, 1995[23]; Hannon et al., 2006[24]; Sylva et al., 2004[25]).

Emergence

'Emergence' is a philosophical notion that dates back to the earliest writings in the 19th Century psychology, and also to classical views of society seen as itself a living organism (Sawyer, 2003)[26].

When the term is applied to early childhood learning and development it suggests that the cognitive structures that emerge in children are irreducible to their component parts. This notion of 'emergence' was an underlying assumption in the developmental psychologies' of both Piaget and Vygotsky (Sawyer, 2003)[26]. 'Emergent Literacy' was a term first applied in Marie Clay's doctoral dissertation (Clay, 1966)[27], and Sulzby and Teale (1991, p.849)[28] defined the concept as:

> [...] the skills, knowledge, and attitudes that are presumed to be developmental precursors to conventional forms of reading and writing, as well as; [...] the environments that support these developments.

Many Apps and online games are available to teach children 'phonics', the letter sounds, and there is some evidence that this might support them in learning to read. Good examples include Ladybird's 'I'm Ready for Phonics' (available for Android and iOS) and BBC's Cbeebies 'Alphablocks' (http://www.bbc.co.uk/cbeebies/grownups/about/programmes/alphablocks.shtml). Siraj-Blatchford and Parmar (2011)[29] have argued that many concerns regarding the use of phonics instruction are relegated to the pedagogy of instruction rather than the content, and that phonics education provided through a playful pedagogy may be beneficial.

But it is important to understand that you cannot teach a child to read just by teaching them the letter sounds. This is because reading is a two-way process and the reader must recognise individual letters that form words, and build their understanding of these words in a given context. This involves two different competencies, engaging the word processing centres as well as the memory centres of the brain. When we read, we 'communicate' with the writer. We try to interpret what they have written, and create our own images, whereas a viewer of a movie, for example, plays a more passive role when watching the film.

Additionally, we use other significant strategies to recognise words in reading, and in pre-schools it is important that we support children in their use of all of these strategies, and not just through teaching them letter sounds. When we read we typically skip over 15% of all content words (nouns, verbs, adjectives and adverbs) and 65% of all function words (prepositions, conjunctions, articles, and pronouns (Paulson & Freeman, 2003)[30].

Computational thinking in early childhood

The importance of children making things has long been recognised in Early Childhood Education. Rousseau[31] suggested in Emile, in 1762:

If, instead of making a child stick to his books, I take him to a workshop, his hands work to the advantage of his intellect, he becomes a philosopher while he thinks he is simply becoming an artisan [...].

The same principle was fundamental to Fröbel (1826)[32] who provided the foundations of our modern kindergarten and play based early education system. Fröbel argued that engaging children in making things served to develop the whole child. He believed that creative activity provided both a means of expression and a powerful context within which children would develop essential habits of thought that included:

[...] success, a calm sense of power, a firm conviction of mastership, which are so essential to fullness of life [...] (Hailman, 1887, p.37)[33].

According to Archer (1986)[34] the more academic bias of our education system may actually be the result of a historical misunderstanding of a statement about the essentials of education that dates back at least to the time of Saint Augustine, and the 4th Century Roman Empire (Pusey, 1896)[35]. Since the early 19th Century we have seen an educational emphasis being placed on the so-called phonemic three R's of 'Reading, Writing and Arithmentic'. We do not know if this version of the three R's represents an adaptation, or if its original meaning was simply lost in translation from the Latin, but education was apparently first understood as requiring a balance between (Williams, 2012)[36]:

- reading and writing (literacy),

- reckoning (arithmetic, precision and judgement), and

- wroughting (making things).

Ruskin (1857)[37] clearly recognised this need for balance in education, when he wrote that you have: "the head, the heart and the hand, and thus you produce the complete person".

In 2014 in England, the national curriculum for Information and Communications Technology (ICT) was scrapped, as it was widely recognised as inadequate in keeping pace with technological developments. In its place, schools were provided with a new national curriculum for 'Computing'. While a significant emphasis of the old ICT curriculum was on the application of technology, the core of this new subject of computing is computer science. This provides a welcome return to emphasising 'making' rather than simply using technology. In this new school curriculum pupils are taught the principles of:

Computational Thinking (CT)

Computational thinking (CT) is: "[...] a mode of thought that goes well beyond software and hardware, and that provides a framework within which to reason about systems and problems" (Computing At School, 2011)[38]. In fact CT involves concepts and skills that lie at the heart of computing, such as thinking in the abstract, the decomposition of problems, pattern matching, generalisation, inference and algorithm design.

Children can learn decomposition (breaking systems down into components) at an early age, e.g. in identifying the different stages of activity (the 'algorithm') involved in making a cake:

- Get ingredients.
- Combine ingredients.
- Put in pan.
- Bake in oven.
- Let cool.
- Decorate.

To take this example further, we can consider a particular cake 'program' that would provide a specific realisation of the algorithm (a recipe):

- Preheat oven.

- Take 4oz of butter, 4oz of self raising flour and 4oz of sugar.

- Rub the ingredients together in a large bowl.

- Fold in 2 beaten eggs, and then continue beating until you have a smooth and soft batter.

- Pour into 2 round sandwich tins.

- Bake in 190°C fan oven for 20-25 minutes until golden.

- Remove from pan and let cool on cooling racks.

In fact, in many countries around the world, computing and 'computational thinking' have been included in early childhood education for many years. A decade and a half ago, the Early Learning Goals in the Curriculum Guidance for the Foundation Stage in England suggested that, before children entered primary school, they should "find out about and identify the uses of technology in their everyday lives and use computers and programmed toys to support their learning". Teachers were also advised that settings should "encourage children to observe and talk about the use of ICT in the environment on local walks, for example traffic lights, telephones, street lights, bar-code scanners to identify prices in shops"; and they should "encourage children to show each other how to use ICT equipment" (DfEE/QCA, 2000)[39].

- information and computation (making sense of data and working things out),

- how digital systems work (through the use of Os and 1s), and

- how to put this knowledge to use through programming (designing a series of instructions to make something happen successfully).

The overall aim of a computing curriculum is that pupils become digitally literate: 'able to use, and express themselves and develop their ideas through, information and communication technology' (Department of Education, 2013)[40]. A major objective is also to promote 'Computational Thinking', for children to learn to model problems in a way that makes them open to computational solutions. To understand what is intended here we might consider an everyday pre-school activity such as tidying up the sand play area. When computational thinking is applied to this kind of activity, it becomes a process that is carried out by a single or group of human 'processors' interacting with other systems to achieve their goal. The process has a 'start state' (the sand spilt on the floor, toys scattered, cover off the box) and an 'end state' (sand back in the box, toys put away, lid on box) – and the procedure for getting from the start state to the end state can be described by a set of instructions (an algorithm) that is executed by the person or persons doing

Children's early learning about programming begins with learning about switching 'things' on and off, and progresses towards learning about programmes and programming (i.e. how things are switched on and off in sequence).

A simple and familiar example to most readers is the programme that runs in a domestic washing machine.

Washing machine programmes initially involved mechanical switching like Charles Babbage's 19th century 'Difference Engine', which provided an important stage in the development of the historical development of the first computers.

Washing machines may now be controlled by electronic microprocessors but the programmes function in the same way:

> On loading your clothes into a washing machine, you are usually required to select a 'program' that is determined by your decisions regarding the size of the load, the appropriate temperature of the water for the wash and rinse cycles, the length of these cycles, and the speed of agitation, and of the final spin. These decisions will in part depend upon the strength and nature of the fabrics that are to be washed (e.g. if they are delicate, woollen, dyed and heavy, etc.), and on how soiled your clothes are. The choices that the operator has to make are often simplified according to the most common loads likely to be considered. After you fill the tub with clothes and switch on the programme it is executed; a valve first opens to allow the machine to fill with water and then a heating element is switched on. As soon as the machine senses that it is full the valve is closed, and when it reaches the appropriate temperature the heating element is switched off as well. Then the clothes are stirred (or rolled) around by the agitator. After an appropriate period (and quality) of agitating, the drain valve is then opened and the water pumped out, and the machine then spins the clothes to remove most of the water. It refills, and agitates the clothes again to rinse out the soap. Then it drains and it spins again (Siraj-Blatchford & Whitebread, 2003)[41].

It is important to recognise that tablets, laptops and desktop computers, and the microprocessors, including programmable toys, mobile phones, game consoles and washing machines, etc. (the list is endless), are simply mass produced electronic devices that are controlled by (or follow) their programs. It is their programs that significantly distinguish them and it is their programming that contributes most significantly to their effectiveness and improvement.

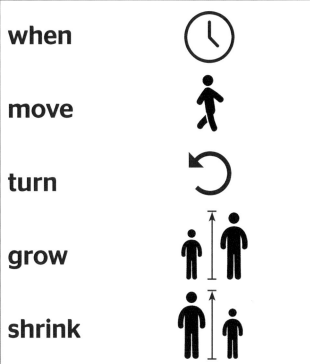

the tiding up (the processor). Your choice of algorithm to get from the given start state to the required end state may depend on a variety of factors, including the capabilities of the processor (what instructions the child or children will understand), the availability of resources (dustpan and brush), and constraints such as the number of processors available, and the time available to complete the task. In supporting CT in the pre-school the teacher may develop the algorithm with the children, identifying the essential features of the problem to be solved, using modelling, block diagrams and/or story boards.

Programming 'problems' may be set for programmable toys. For example, in one pre-school, following a visit by the children to local shops, landmarks and features taking photographs, the staff and children created a 'mat' and the children programmed their toy to follow the route of the postman delivering letters. Readymade 'mats' are available from Technology Teaching systems (TTS) to support children's learning with Bee-Bot®.

In addition to programmable toys (e.g. Bee-Bot®) and the associated on-screen 'turtle' Apps (e.g. Bee-Bot™ and Move the Turtle™) and programs now available, there are Apps specifically developed to teach the principles of programming. Notable among these for early childhood use are Daisy the Dinosaur™, Cargo Bot™ and ScratchJr™. Other Apps requiring rather more support from more capable siblings or adults in early childhood include Hopscotch™ and Kodable™.

Daisy the Dinosaur™ is typical of the genre. It is very intuitive, and offers a first taste of computer programming. 'Daisy' supports children in developing perseverance, problem-solving and analytical skills. The youngest children will need help with reading the commands, and may benefit from a supporting visual display that illustrates the commands that are available.

The activities on Daisy the Dinosaur™ progress to demonstrate looping and conditional programming. In the 'Free Play' mode, adults can create programming challenges for the children. Cargo Bot™ and ScratchJr™ use symbols, but the programming for Cargo Bot™ and the others is more challenging and adult support is needed. It is important to remember that this is not a disadvantage, as this may maximise the 'sustained shared thinking' (see Literacy and Early Learning section). ScratchJr™ has enormous potential for young children and you can access valuable activity guides on YouTube.

Conceptual learning

If we are to fully appreciate the importance and value of computational thinking in early childhood education we must first consider some established principles of child development and learning. Firstly, it is important to distinguish between the relatively trivial learning involved in associating particular words or names to the everyday people, objects, and phenomenon that we encounter in our environment. Then there is the more challenging conceptual learning that requires the development of understanding. When educators apply the theories of Piaget and Vygotsky to say that early childhood education should be 'child centred', they are drawing attention to the fact that whenever a child develops a new understanding of something, they are engaged in an interpretive, creative and constructive process.

Learning is always a creative process whether it leads us to established shared understandings, or alternative ones, and in the early years, learning is essential to child development. Our capability to control our imagination is something that develops over our lifetime; it's a bit like juggling. As we get older and more experienced, we can handle more abstract concepts, such as the relationships between some variables in Mathematics and Physics. For example, the relationship between area, length and width in mathematics; between pressure, temperature and volume in Boyles Law, and voltage, resistance and current in Ohms Law. Manipulating three related variables is a bit like juggling three (imaginary) balls in the air, and by age 11 or 12 many of us are capable of it. The kinds of problems we are often faced with in social, cultural, economic and environmental decision-making have even more variables, without even considering personal and professional relationships.

Conceptual learning begins at an early age when we first begin placing things into categories, e.g. when we distinguish

between the significant males and females in our lives, and between family and friends. When we first learn the names of different flowers; rose, daffodil, daisy for example; the word 'flower' is at first interchangeable with each of them. But at some point, perhaps in the context of encountering them combined in a vase or bouquet, the child will learn that the word flower also provides a conceptual category. In most cases this concept will develop much further in the process of the child's education so that they become aware of the overall reproductive function of flowers and the more specific functions of the different parts that they share, the (petals, carpels and stamen, etc.). If they take a special interest, or become a professional botanist the concept may eventually become very elaborate.

For van Oers (1998)[42], the creative processes that are involved in these kinds of learning and development may be characterised as a process of 'progressive continuous re-contextualisation'. For Vygotsky, creative activity was seen as combinational activity, where the individual brings together recalled images, actions and/or experiences to envisage (or imagine) something new. These processes of imagination are present in all aspects of our day to day life and mental activity. In fact, all forms of learning, Science and Technology, just as much as Art, would be impossible without them:

> [...] in the everyday life that surrounds us, creativity is an essential condition for existence and all that goes beyond the rut of routine and involves innovation, albeit only a tiny amount, owes its existence to the human creative process (Vygotsky, 2004, p.11).[43]

Creative learning and schemes

A good way to understand the development of young children's creativity is to consider it in terms of the development and manipulation of 'schemes' (Siraj-Blatchford, 2004[44]; Siraj-Blatchford & Brock, 2015[45]). For Piaget (1969)[46] and other developmental psychologists, a scheme is understood as an 'operational thought'. It may be a recalled behaviour, the recollection of a single action, or a sequence of actions. To be creative, children need to acquire a repertoire of schemes, and they also need the playful disposition to try out these schemes in new contexts. These trials may be expressed verbally, in their imagination, or in the material world. Young children are naturally curious and they learn many of their schemes vicariously; they spontaneously imitate a wide range of the schemes provided by adults and other children.

In their fantasy play, young children quite naturally separate objects and actions from their meaning in the real world and give them new meanings. They should be encouraged to communicate these creative representations because it is in this way that their powers of expression and abstraction may be developed more generally (van Oers, 1999)[11]. Educators may encourage the discovery of such schemes, and provide explicit models for the children to follow in their play. Early childhood development may usefully be considered to involve progression in the child's capabilities in terms of schemes and abstract thinking. One of the key tasks for an educator then becomes: how can we support children in developing these transferable and essential skills of abstraction? The answer is that we can draw upon their natural desire to play – 'playing with ideas'. Education for 'computational thinking' has a significant role to play involving structured play with construction toys and bricks, activities such as breaking down stories into story boards and then building them up again, adapting them, creating new ones. One of the most valuable skills being learnt by the child along the way is the motivation to stay on task to achieve much more with adult support than they ever imagined possible.

The EYFS characteristics of early learning can be downloaded for free from the Foundation Years website (see: http://www.foundationyears.org.uk/files/2012/03/Development-Matters-FINAL-PRINT-AMENDED.pdf).

Utilising 'Apps' for learning

Short for applications, 'Apps' are software programmes that can be downloaded onto a mobile device. Apps have become commonplace in pre- and primary schools, homes and informal learning environments, due mainly to their relative low cost, the ubiquity of mobile technologies and their general popularity among young children and adults. Young children respond to these tools with remarkable capability, and since early 2010 the tablet App market has burgeoned, with mobile App revenue worldwide expected to generate $38 billion by 2015. However, to date, little research has been undertaken to evaluate the influence that Apps might have on children's learning and development.

Furthermore, in light of the 100,000s of Apps marketed as educational, criticisms have been raised about the challenges confronting parents and educators when navigating the complex and constantly evolving children's App market. There is also a lack of official guidance and criteria for developmentally appropriate Apps.

What do teachers and parents need to bear in mind when choosing Apps for learning?

Firstly, don't just think about using an App for its own sake. Think about the specific activity that you wish to use it for, what it is that you want the child to learn from it, and then how an App might fit into that activity. How might using an App, for example counting, extend children's knowledge and skills? Or for creative Apps, for example a drawing App, think about how that drawing App might encourage the child's creativity and/or their knowledge of colours and shapes.

Creativity

It is widely accepted that we should distinguish between personal creativity and self-expression on the one hand, and the kind of creativity that contributes historically to cultural achievements (Boden, 2004)[47]. The contrast of terms "Big C" Creativity and "Little c" creativity has been widely used (Craft, 2001)[48]. Kaufman and Beghetto (2009)[49] introduced a "four C" model of creativity; mini-c creativity that involves "personally meaningful interpretations of experiences, actions and insights", little-c creativity, our everyday problem solving and creative expression, Pro-C creativity which is exhibited by people who are professionally or vocationally creative though not necessarily eminent and Big-C creativity. This model was intended to help accommodate models and theories of creativity that stressed competence as an essential component, and the historical transformation of a creative domain as the highest mark of creativity.

The creativity that we refer to here is the mini-c kind that is hard-wired into every child and which they apply from birth in their active learning. This conception is consistent with Runco's (2004)[50] description of "personal creativity", and is also similar to Niu and Sternberg's (2006)[51] notion of "individual creativity," and developmental conceptions of creativity (Beghetto & Plucker, 2006[52]; Cohen, 1989[53]; Sawyer et al., 2003[54]; Vygotsky, 2004[43]).

If the App comes with some open-ended drawing possibilities, then the child will have more creative opportunities than with a template-based App offering only pre-established patterns and a set of colours. You may find it useful to think about how you encourage creativity and at different times, how you encourage the child's self-expression.

Secondly, follow some general rules of thumb for appropriate resources for young children: the App should facilitate safe and playful learning, in front of and away from the screen, interactive and shared engagement, creativity and personalisation. You can draw inspiration from some of the review sites available online, for example Moms with Apps (https://www.momswithApps.com/) or Apps playground (http://Appsplayground.com/), or discuss them with other parents, teachers and the children themselves (see Choosing the right resources section).

Thirdly, think about whether the App enriches the off-screen version of an activity. A literacy App may link a physical book with an audio narration, and a drama activity. A counting App might encourage the child to count objects in a construction activity. A science App might encourage children to discover some information about the trees in their local park. The more children can make a connection between the content in the App and their own lives, the more they will learn.

Finally, the best children's Apps are those which enhance relationships and encourage children to think about others. For example, a story-making App can be used to create and share a shared experience or story; a counting App can be linked to a social game where several users solve problems together. Children need to learn from early on that technologies encourage active creation and sharing with others.

References

1   Snow, C., Burns, M., & Griffin, P. (1998). *Preventing Reading Difficulties in Young Children*. Washington, DC: National Academy Press.

2   Hart, B., & Risley, T.R. (1995). *Meaningful Differences in the Everyday Experience of Young American Children*. Baltimore, MD: Brookes.

3   Waldfogel, J., & Washbrook, E. (2010). *Low Income and Early Cognitive Development in the UK*. London: The Sutton Trust.

4   Mansell, W. (2010). Poor children a year behind in language skills. *The Guardian*, 15th February 2010. Available at: http://www.theguardian.com/education/2010/feb/15/poor-children-behind-sutton-trust

5   Siraj-Blatchford, I., Sylva, K., Muttock, S., Gilden, R., & Bell, D. (2002). *Researching Effective Pedagogy in the Early Years (REPEY) DfES Research Report 365*. HMSO London: Queen's Printer.

6   Siraj-Blatchford, I. (2007). Creativity, communication and collaboration: The identification of pedagogic progression in sustained shared thinking. *Asia-Pacific Journal of Research in Early Childhood Education*, 1(2), 3-23.

7   It might also be considered to be childhood 'social life phases' (see Higgins & Eccles-Parson, 1983).

8   Lisina, A. (1986). *Problems of the Ontogenesis of Communication*. Moscow: Pedagogika.

9   Elkonin, D. (1989). *Selected Psychological Works*. Moscow: Pedagogika.

10 Leontiev, A. (1964). *Problems of Mental Development*. Washington: US Joint Publication Research Service.

11 van Oers, B. (1999). Teaching opportunities in play. In M. Hedegaard, & J. Lompscher (Eds.), *Learning Activity and Development* (pp. 268-289). Aarhus: Aarhus University Press.

12 United Nations Educational, Scientific and Cultural Organisation (UNESCO) (2014). Reading in the Mobile Era. Available at: http://www.unesco.org/new/en/unesco/themes/icts/single-view/news/reading_in_the_mobile_era/#.VFCz4WeuvKd

13 e-Skills UK (2014). The Women in IT Scoreboard. Swindon: BCS The Chartered Institute for ICT. Available at: http://www.e-skills.com/Documents/Research/General/WomeninIT_Scorecard_Jun14.pdf

14 The Office of Communications (OFCOM) (2013). 2013 *Children and parents: Media use and attitudes report*. Available at: http://stakeholders.ofcom.org.uk/binaries/research/media-literacy/october2013/research07Oct2013.pdf

15 Siraj-Blatchford, J., & Whitebread, D. (2003). *Supporting Information and Communications Technology in the Early Years*. Buckingham: Open University Press.

16 Laurel, B. (1990). *The Art of Human-Computer Interface Design*. Chichester: Ellis Harwood.

17 Epstein, D. (1995). Girls don't do bricks: Gender and sexuality in the primary classroom. In J. Siraj-Blatchford, & I. Siraj-Blatchford (Eds.), *Educating the Whole Child: Cross Curriculum Skills, Themes and Dimensions* (pp. 56-69). Buckingham: Open University Press.

18 Brooker, E., & Siraj-Blatchford, J. (2002). 'Click on Miaow!': How children of 3 and 4 experience the nursery computer. *Journal of Contemporary Issues in Early Education*, 3(2), 251-273.

19 Freedman, T. (2012). Digital literacy and computer science. ICT in Education. Available at: http://www.ictineducation.org/home-page/2012/1/19/digital-literacy-and-computer-science.html

20 Rogoff, B. (2003). *The Cultural Nature of Human Development*. New York: Oxford University Press.

21 Vygotsky, L.S. (1978). *Mind in Society: The Development of Higher Psychological Processes*. Cambridge, MA: Harvard University Press.

22 Bodrova, E., & Leong, D.J. (2007). *Tools of the Mind: The Vygotskian Approach to Early Childhood Education (2nd ed.)*. Columbus, OH: Merrill/Prentice Hall.

23 Hannon, P. (1995). *Literacy, Home and School: Research and Practice in Teaching Literacy with Parents*. London: Falmer Press.

24 Hannon, P., Morgan, A., & Nutbrown, C. (2006). Parents' experiences of a family literacy programme. *Journal of Early Childhood Research*, 4(1), 19-44.

25 Sylva, K., Melhuish, E.C., Sammons, P., Siraj, I., & Taggart, B. (2004). *The Effective Provision of Pre-School Education (EPPE) Project: Technical Paper 12-The Final Report: Effective Pre-School Education*. London: DfES/Institute of Education, University of London.

26 Sawyer, R. (2003). Emergence in creativity & development. In R. Sawyer, V. J. Steiner, S. Moran, & D. Feldman (Eds.), *Creativity & Development* (pp. 12-60). Oxford: Oxford University Press.

27 Clay, M. (1966). *Emergent reading behavior*. Unpublished doctoral dissertation, University of Auckland, New Zealand.

28 Sulzby, E., & Teale, W. (1991). Emergent literacy. In R. Barr, M.L. Kamil, P.B. Mosenthal, & P.D. Pearson (Eds.), *Handbook of Reading Research* (vol. 2, pp. 727-757). New York: Longman.

29 Siraj-Blatchford, J., & Parmar, N. (2011). *Knowledge learning processes and ICT in early childhood education*. He Kupu, 2(5), 45–60.

30 Paulson, E.J., & Freeman, A.E. (2003). *Insight from the Eyes: The Science of Effective Reading Instruction*. Portsmouth, NH: Heinemann Educational Books.

31 Rousseau, J.J. (1762). *Emile*. CreateSpace IPP.

32 Fröbel, F. (1826). *The Education of Man*. New York: D. Appleton Century.

33 Hailman, W. [Translator] (1887). Fröbel, F. *The Education of Man*. New York: D. Appleton Century.

34 Archer, B. (1986). The three R's in technology in schools. In A. Cross, & B. McCormick (Eds.), *Technology in Schools* (pp. 49–56). Milton Keynes: The Open University.

35 Pusey, E. [Translator] (1896). *The Confessions of Saint Augustine*. CreateSpace IPP.

36 Williams, P.J. (Ed.) (2012). *Technology Education for Teachers*. Rotterdam: Sense Publishers.

37 Ruskin, J. (1857). A joy for ever (and its price in the market). In E. Cook, & A. Wedderburn (Eds.), *The Complete Works of John Ruskin*. London: George Allen.

38 Computing At School (2011). *Computing: A curriculum for schools*. Available at: http://csta.acm.org/Curriculum/sub/CurrFiles/CASUKComputingCurric.pdf

39 DfEE/QCA (2000). *Curriculum Guidance for the Foundation Stage*. London: DfEE/QCA.

40 Department of Education (2013). *Computing programmes of study: Key stages 1 and 2. National Curriculum in England*. Available at: http://www.computingatschool.org.uk/data/uploads/primary_national_curriculum_-_computing.pdf

41 Siraj-Blatchford, J., & Whitebread, D. (2003). *Supporting Information and Communications Technology in the Early Years*. Buckingham: Open University Press.

42 van Oers, B. (1998). The fallacy of decontextualisatoin. *Mind, Culture & Activity*, 5(2), 135–142.

43 Vygotsky, L. (2004). Imagination & creativity in childhood. *Journal of Russian & East European Psychology*, 42(1), 4–84.

44 Siraj-Blatchford, J. (2004). *Developing New Technologies for Young Children*. Stoke on Trent: Trentham Books.

45 Siraj-Blatchford, J., & Brock, L. (2015). *Investigating schemes and schema in emergent mathematics*. Paper presented at TACTYC Conference 2015. Birmingham.

46 Piaget, J. (1969). *The Mechanisms of Perception*. New York: Basic Books.

47 Boden, M.A. (2004). *The Creative Mind: Myths and Mechanisms*. London: Routledge.

48 Craft, A. (2001). Little c creativity. In A. Craft, R. Jeffrey, & M. Leibling (Eds.), *Creativity in Education* (pp. 45–61). London: Continuum.

49 Kaufman, J.C., & Beghetto, R.A. (2009). Beyond big and little: The four C model of creativity. *Review of General Psychology*, 13(1), 1–12.

50 Runco, M.A. (2004). Personal creativity and culture. In S. Lau, A.N.N. Hui, & G.Y.C. Ng (Eds.), *Creativity When East Meets West* (pp. 9–22). New Jersey: World Scientific.

51 Niu, W., & Sternberg, R. (2006). The philosophical roots of Western and Eastern conceptions of creativity. *Journal of Theoretical and Philosophical Psychology*, 26(1-2), 18–38.

52 Beghetto, R.A., & Plucker, J.A. (2006). The relationship among schooling, learning, and creativity: "All roads lead to creativity" or "you can't get there from here"? In J. C. Kaufman, & J. Baer (Eds.), *Creativity and Reason in Cognitive Development* (pp. 316–332). Cambridge: Cambridge University Press.

53 Cohen, L.M. (1989). A continuum of adaptive creative behaviors. *Creativity Research Journal*, 2(3), 169–183.

54 Sawyer, R.K., John-Steiner, V., Moran, S., Sternberg, R. J., Feldman, D.H., Nakamura, J., & Csikszentmihalyi, M. (2003). *Creativity and Development*. New York: Oxford University Press.

Peer-to-peer play

Play is a crucial element of young children's lives. It nurtures children's creativity, imagination and provides the context within which they explore and gain their first understandings of the world. Children's playful learning can be enhanced not only through adult guidance but also in collaboration with more knowledgeable peers (Vygotsky, 1978)[1]. In sustained shared thinking (Siraj-Blatchford, 2007)[2], children work together with peers or adults in an intellectual way to solve a problem, clarify a concept, evaluate activities or extend a narrative. This chapter focuses on peer-to-peer play.

Bandura's (1977)[3] theory of learning emphasises the way in which children learn through watching other children and adults, who provide model behaviours for the child. Vygotsky's (1978)[1] sociocultural perspective shows how a more knowledgeable/ capable peer can provide practical assistance, demonstrations, explanations, questions, corrections and other interactions, to enable a child to achieve more than what they can do by themselves. In education this is referred to as 'scaffolding'.

What does the research say about peer engagement with ICT?

One of the concerns about children using ICT focuses on their becoming isolated from social interactions. However, research has shown that when used effectively, ICT can support children's social-emotional development (Clements & Sarama, 2003[4]; McCarrick & Li, 2007[5]) and encourage cooperation, collaboration and competition among children. Various types of peer collaboration through ICT have been observed in our previous research. These included: joint planning; taking turns; asking for and providing opinions; sharing, chaining and integrating of ideas; arguing their points of view; negotiating and coordinating perspectives; adding, revising, reformulating and elaborating on the information under discussion and seeking of agreements (Rojas-Drummond et al., 2008[6]; Kucirkova et al., 2014[7]).

Recently, some research has focused on the quality of children's talk when using iPad Apps. Kucirkova et al. (2014)[7] and Falloon and Khoo (2014)[8] showed that Apps of an open design provide valuable opportunities for exploratory talks among four- to five-year-old children, which further help support their critical thinking and reasoning capabilities in the classroom. The open-ended Apps used in the research included: Puppet Pals HD™, Pic Collage™, Popplet™ and Our Story™. Another feature common to these Apps is their support for content creation, which is different from a passive consumption design.

It is worth noting that not all children equally engage in shared activities. Ljung-Djärf (2004)[9] has observed three distinct roles of children around desktop computers in order of their involvement in the activity: the owner, the participant and the spectator.

In the research of Bangert-Drowns and Pyke (2001)[10], seven different forms of student engagement with educational software were identified in order of complexity: disengagement, unsystematic engagement, frustrated engagement, structure-dependent engagement, self-regulated interest, critical engagement, and literate thinking (see Table 1).

Scaffolding

Bruner (1996)[11] and Wood et al. (1976)[12] applied the term 'scaffolding' to indicate the processes whereby adults provide support, and then gradually withdraw this, as the children become more capable. From a scaffolding perspective, the aim of the educator is to provide the support and encouragement the child requires to perform successfully in areas that would otherwise be beyond their capabilities. Adapting Smith's (1994)[13] account, scaffolding may involve:

- an adult or another child drawing attention to something otherwise missed,
- helping the child break down a task into a sequence of smaller tasks which are more manageable, and
- helping the child to sequence steps in the right order.

Rogoff (2003)[14] has identified three distinct forms that scaffolding can take:

- the community learning processes of Apprenticeship that often entail explicit teaching,
- the interpersonal processes of Guided participation that are (for example) most significant in practitioners support of children during their play, and
- the personal learning processes of Appropriation whereby the child takes what they have learnt and transfers this learning to another time and place.

Table 1 Seven levels of student engagement with educational software (Source: Bangert-Drowns & Pyke, 2001)[10]

Taxonomy Level	Level Description
Literate thinking	Student interprets software content from multiple and personally meaningful perspectives. Student manipulates software features to explore alternative interpretations as an opportunity to reflect on personal values or experiences.
Critical engagement	Student investigates operational and content-related limitations of the software. Student manipulates software features to test personal understandings or limitations of the software presentations.
Self-regulated interest	Student creates per make the software as personally interesting as possible. Student adjusts software features to sustain deeply involved, interesting, or challenging interactions. Student adapts software for personally defined purposes.
Structure dependent engagement	Student is sensitive to and competent with software operation and navigation. Student pursues goals communicated by the software and responds to operational, navigational, or content organisation.
Frustrated engagement	Student possesses clear goals when working with the software but is unsuccessful in accomplishing them. Student knows what the software can do, but cannot accomplish it. Student may manifest stress or frustration in negative comments, confusion, aggression, erratic behaviour, agitation, distress, or anxiety.
Unsystematic engagement	Student has unclear goals when working with the software. Student moves from one incomplete activity to another without apparent reason. Student successfully completes simple tasks within the software but does not link tasks for higher-order goals.
Disengagement	Student avoids working with the software or discontinues use prematurely. Student may tinker with software in a seemingly purposeless and unresponsive way. Or, student may in fact turn away from the software or resist using it at all.

How to choose the right resource for peer-to-peer play

Many Apps that claim to be 'educational' in the market fail to achieve their intended goals. Facing a rapidly growing number of Apps, how to choose the right resources for young children has become a tricky, yet important, task for caregivers. Some Apps are designed to support adult-child play, some are suitable for peer-to-peer play, and some are for independent use. Of particular relevance to supporting peer-to-peer play is the multi-user accessible interface offered by some Apps (e.g. Finger Paint With Sounds™). As a starting point, caregivers should choose the right Apps based on children's ages, abilities, interests, and intended learning outcomes.

How to use ICT with (a big group of) children in libraries or classrooms

It is clear that the quality of App content and design can influence children's learning outcomes. While a lot of research has been concerned with children's learning and interactions with Apps, less is known about the practical ways in which Apps can be implemented in the classroom. In the next section, we outline a step-by-step process for integrating Apps into current practice.

Preparation

Apps can be used in their own right or can be incorporated into traditional classroom or library activities to support children's learning experiences. Either way, careful planning and preparation is required to maximise children's learning outcomes. It is essential that caregivers identify the educational goals they wish to achieve with specific Apps. Based on these goals, they need to select relevant Apps, familiarise themselves with the navigation of Apps selected, apply evidence-based instructional techniques to the usage of Apps, and plan data collection methods for evaluation.

Room setup and equipment

Basic equipment for using Apps for demonstration with a big group of children and caregivers (approximately 20 people or more) in the library or classroom includes:

- smartphones or tablets (making sure the handheld devices are fully charged and Apps are pre-downloaded),

- a projector and big screen (to enhance the vision quality, as the screen of a smartphone/tablet is too small for a big group of children),

- a VGA adaptor (to connect a smartphone/tablet and a projector),

- a microphone (to enhance the sound quality, as the sound of a smartphone/tablet is low for a big group of children), and

- the Internet or Wi-Fi (if needed).

For interactive activities, children and/or their caregivers may be encouraged to participate through using the tablets. However, some libraries may not have enough budget to purchase tablets for all attending participants. Considering the increasing rate of handheld device ownership in each household, it is suggested that parents/children bring their own handheld devices along.

Planning

Ideally, App-based projects for children can be co-designed, involving different stakeholders (e.g. parents, children, librarians, teachers, sometimes even App software developers and researchers). Both the children's and parents' information needs should be considered in the project planning; methods such as interviews, observations, focus groups or informal conversations can be used to identify their information needs. If the project takes place in the library, it is essential to engage with both parents and children in the implementation stage of the project. Through participation, caregivers will be able to observe, imitate and learn from the way in which professional librarians or other parents interact with children and with the Apps.

Evaluation

Feedback on App-based projects can be collected through observations of adult-child and peer-to-peer interactions during the event, and questionnaires or interviews at the end of the event. Both qualitative and quantitative data can be gathered, and evaluation of the feedback collected can then be used to inform the design of future projects/activities. The nature of data collected and the ways in which they are evaluated need to be consistent with the learning outcomes set at the preparation and planning stages.

How to develop children's self-regulation when using ICT

When it comes to using smartphones or tablets with young children, screen time has been a critical issue that is concerning for many parents. Some parents even associate Apps with game addiction and so they ban their children from using handheld devices. Conversely, some parents often use playing with handheld devices as a reward if the child behaves well, finishes a task, or completes homework. Parents need to deal with this issue sensibly or children may become increasingly 'techno-materialistic', to the point of making their personal contribution to family life (in terms of help with routine chores) conditional upon access to smartphone access. Parents may then find themselves providing access to smartphone technologies as a 'reward' for good behaviour and performance in other areas. There needs to be a process of 'negotiation' to balance the amount of time spent with ICT.

Indeed, children need to be taught how to use handheld devices responsibly. The communication of rules at the beginning of any playful activity is key. Instead of banning children from using handheld devices, children need to be educated both about the benefits of effectively using handheld devices, and the risks of misusing them. Children need to agree on the rules around the length of play time and the system of taking turns. When siblings or peers play in pairs, they can remind each other about the time and whose turn it is, and parents can also set an alarm on the handheld device. Consistent with the suggested screen time, pre-school teachers and librarians can limit the time of the App-based projects to one or two hours.

Good practice

Good practice often occurs when older siblings play with younger ones, or children provide scaffolding when they play together with ICT. Not all ICT is designed equally – some is designed to allow multi-user participation more than others. Shared activities around ICT provide children with a good context for encouraging dialogue, having fun, and supporting active learning. This is important because active learning is more effective than passive learning (see Figure 1).

In a world that is changing so quickly, children have to begin to learn how to direct their own learning. Yet most schools around the world continue to foster passive learners, discourage productivity, and fail to teach self-regulation

Figure 1 Active learning vs. passive learning (Dale, E. (1969). *Audiovisual Methods in Teaching*. Holt, Rinehart and Winston: Austin, Texas.)[15]

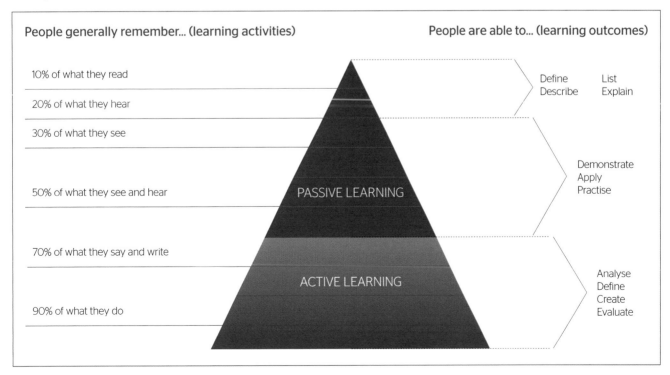

(Nussbaum-Beach, 2015)[16]. The good news is that the best pre-schools do a great deal to promote active learning. Technology can help in providing some of the tools for this but it should not be the primary focus. ICT provides children with the means to capture, share, record and celebrate their observations and discoveries.

Socio-dramatic play

There are various ways in which teachers can promote play with technologies in their classrooms. The benefits of play have been documented by research and involve the ability to develop rules to guide children's actions, shaping these actions as children follow the rules, inhibiting undesired impulses and enabling children to hold complex ideas (Lindon, 2001)[17]. Imaginary play is particularly important for young children's development and is widely considered to be the 'most important "work" of the young child and the activity through which the child grows physically, intellectually, and emotionally' (Edwards, 2002, p.5)[18].

Teachers can support socio-dramatic and imaginary play by including technology in the classroom's role play centres. For example, they can resource role-play areas with cameras and programmable toys to enhance children's imaginary worlds. Children can use these to enact realistic or imaginary roles and assume various roles (for example a photographer when using

the digital camera). Tablet Apps are well suited to support teacher-child imaginary play in virtual worlds. For instance, the My PlayHome Stores™ App allows children to interact with characters and objects in four different imaginary stores. The Toca Pet Doctor™ App presents children with 15 animals who need children's care and attention as if they were real animals.

Children can nurse the animals back to good health by providing them with some bandages or toothbrushes, feeding them or putting them to sleep. Similarly, the Tizzy Veterinarian HD™ App encourages children to care for a selection of sick animals with some more advanced options. Children can choose from a selection of activities, including cleaning, washing, measuring temperature, monitoring blood pressure, feeding and even X-raying the animals. Such activities can provide a great forum for lively dialogue and an opportunity for educators to explain and expand the information embedded in the programmes, and meaningfully link them to children's lives. As children act out their plays, adults can gradually introduce more complex props or digital games and thus build children's cognitive abilities.

Matching games

Matching games are a great method to exercise children's memory. With traditional memory cards, they may be distorted and have marks on the card for children to remember, which to some extent would lose the meaning of the puzzle game. The content on the memory cards is fixed, unless more sets of cards are purchased or prepared and the format is limited to texts and images. The aforementioned limitations of physical memory cards can be solved by using the Bitsboard – Memory Cards™ App, which can help achieve the goal of promoting children's memory and support peer-to-peer play.

The Bitsboard – Memory Cards™ App allows users to choose the content of the memory cards, including ABC (to go with children's literacy training) and 123 and counting (to go with children's numeracy training). Not only does the App provide a wide range of memory card sets to choose from, but it also allows users to personalise the content of the cards. Users can decide the number of players (from one to four) in order for the system to make a record of scores for each person. In terms of complexity levels of the game, users can choose the number of memory cards (from four to 60) and different matching options (e.g. image to image, text to text, image to audio and image to text).

When using the Bitsboard – Memory Cards™ App, children can play individually or in a team. When children play against each other, there are elements of taking turns and competition. When children play in the same team, they help each other through offering tips. All in all, this App has advantages in terms of getting children to think and recollect the positions of the flipped cards, whilst they exercise their memory skills.

Table 2 A boy's narration of the Little Red Riding Hood

Book pages	Boy's narration
	Left Boy: "Once upon a time the Little Red Riding Hood's grandfather passed away. Her grandmother passed his clothes with a red hood to an old lady and asked her to pass the clothes to the Little Red Riding Hood. Right Old lady: "This is the only thing that your grandfather left for you. Please take care of it." Little Red Riding Hood: "Ok. I've got it."
	Left Boy: "Outside the room was a wood-cutter. He worked very hard but he earned very little. He only had water for lunch." Right Wood-cutter: "Erm...."

Dialogic reading

Dialogic reading is an established method to enhance children's learning in the home learning environment. Typical good questions that children are asked when sharing a book include: naming "what's that?" by pointing to objects on the page, predicting "what will happen next?" based on the pictures in the book, and guessing "why" something happens in the story. These can be easily achieved using a physical picture book as a tool. However, ICT can help enhance the reading experience by providing sound effects, animations and a recording function.

In addition to telling stories, the Me Books™ App enables children to define their own recordable hotspots around images in electronic books. Children can add their own sound effects or add dialogue, descriptions or narrative information to the story. Whilst the texts provided in Me Books™ are in English, children can audio record any languages of their choice. Children can also use their imagination to re-create their stories based on the built-in images. This is particularly useful when the book is written in a foreign language to the child's mother tongue and written using a different cultural background from the child's. In this case, children can personalise and localise the story to something with which they are familiar. This has advantages in terms of getting children to think, imagine, relate to their personal experiences, speak, sing, and listen to one another's ideas and narration.

Me Books™ works well when older and younger children play together as there are a wide range of books available and different ways of using this App. For example, a father read the story of Fun at the Fair with his two daughters aged three and four years respectively. One was rather shy and the other was active. When the music was played on the first page, the active girl started to sing "Butterfly, butterfly really pretty. Wearing golden wires on the head, wearing colourful dress on the body [...]." She repeated playing her audio recording to share with her sister.

Another example occurred when an older brother (aged eight years) narrated a story of Little Red Riding Hood to his younger brother (aged four years). The older brother's narration (see Table 2) made his younger brother, as an audience, laugh and request to hear more. The story narrated by the boy was totally different from the original version, but still remained relevant to the protagonist – Little Red Riding Hood.

References

1   Vygotsky, L.S. (1978). *Mind in Society: The Development of Higher Psychological Processes*. Cambridge, MA: Harvard University Press.

2   Siraj-Blatchford, I. (2007). Creativity, communication and collaboration: The identification of pedagogic progression in sustained shared thinking. *Asia-Pacific Journal of Research in Early Childhood Education*, 1(2), 3–23.

3   Bandura, A. (1977). *Social Learning Theory*. Englewood Cliffs, NJ: Prentice Hall.

4   Clements, D.H., & Sarama, J. (2003). Strip mining for gold: Research and policy in educational technology: A response to "Fool's Gold". *AACE Journal*, 11(1), 7–69.

5   McCarrick, K., & Li, X. (2007). Buried treasure: The impact of computer use on young children's social, cognitive, language development and motivation. *AACE Journal*, 15(1), 73–95.

6   Rojas-Drummond, S.M., Albarrán, C.D., & Littleton, K. (2008). Collaboration, creativity and the co-construction of oral and written texts. *Thinking Skills and Creativity*, 3(3), 177–191.

7   Kucirkova, N., Messer, D., Sheehy, K., & Fernández, P.C. (2014). Children's engagement with educational iPad apps: Insights from a Spanish classroom. *Computers & Education*, 71, 175–184.

8   Falloon, G., & Khoo, E. (2014). Exploring young students' talk in iPad-supported collaborative learning environments. *Computers & Education*, 77, 13–28.

9   Ljung-Djärf, A. (2004). *Play around the Computer: Computer Use as Meaning-shaping Practice in Pre-school*. Malmö: Malmö University, School of Education.

10 Bangert-Drowns, R.L., & Pyke, C. (2001). A taxonomy of student engagement with educational software: An exploration of literate thinking with electronic text. *Journal of Educational Computing Research*, 24(3), 213–234.

11 Bruner, J. (1996). *The Culture of Education*. Cambridge, MA: Harvard University Press.

12 Wood, D., Bruner, J.S., & Ross, G. (1976). The role of tutoring in problem solving. *Journal of Child Psychology and Psychiatry*, 17(2), 89–100.

13 Smith, P.K. (1994). Play and the uses of play. In J. Moyles (Ed.), *The Excellence of Play* (pp. 15–17). Buckingham: Open University Press.

14 Rogoff, B. (2003). *The Cultural Nature of Human Development*. New York: Oxford University Press.

15 Dale, E. (1969). *Audiovisual Methods in Teaching*. Holt, Rinehart and Winston: Austin, Texas.

16 Nussbaum-Beach, S. (2015). *The key to making the shift to active learning (and why technology is not enough)*. Available at: http://plpnetwork.com/2015/03/10/shift-active-learning-technology-answer/

17 Lindon, J. (2001). *Understanding Children's Play*. Cheltenham: Nelson Thornes.

18 Edwards, C.P. (2002). Three approaches from Europe: Waldorf, Montessori, and Reggio Emilia. *Early Childhood Research & Practice*, 4(1). Available at: http://www.ecrp.uiuc.edu/v4n1/edwards.html

Adult-child play

Play typically offers many and varied benefits, including introducing children to new concepts, enabling them to practise adult roles, and gaining confidence and understanding of the world. Through these experiences, children learn new ideas, skills and ways to problem-solve.

Adults can support children's learning through play by providing a range of resources that facilitate creative and active exploration, whether this is indoors or outdoors. In this chapter we will focus on adult-child play and the various ways in which adults can join children in different play activities, enhancing the children's learning experience without necessarily 'instructing' or 'taking over'.

We will also look at advice on best practice, including the benefits of active engagement with technology and parent-child co-viewing.

Parental involvement in children's play

There is a body of research that shows that parental involvement in children's activities is vital for children's learning and healthy development. In the 1980s, Seitz, Rosenbaum and Apfel[1] found that parental support at home can significantly benefit children. One of the UK's largest studies focusing on the provision of education for young children, the Effective Pre-school Provision Education (EPPE) found that the level of support parents provide at home is more important than their educational status or occupation (Melhuish et al. 2001[2]. The study looked at 3,000 children across the UK, and this has become a key finding for parents who are keen to support children in their learning and school environment.

Parents' and children's use of technology at home

Technology develops dynamically and rapidly, and ICT research often cannot keep up with the pace of technology change. However, there is converging research evidence on the importance of joint parent-child engagement with a piece of technology, often referred to as cooperative 'co-viewing' or 'co-playing'.

Research on joint parent-child media engagement dates back to educational TV content and a body of work conducted by the researchers involved with the TV programme Sesame Street (broadcast both in the US and the UK). The researchers found that children whose parents talk about the show as they watch it learn more from the programme than those who do not.[3] This is because parents or caregivers who co-view TV with their children can guide their attention to salient features of the programme, and they can link the content to children's own lives and help them make meaning of it. This is not unique to TV – the importance of parent-child co-viewing is paramount in ensuring that children get the most out of their playful engagement with Apps, Wiis or any other gadget they may have at home. In addition to TV and computers, many children have access to iPads, smartphones, Wiis, leapsters or programmable toys at home (Plowman, McPake, & Stephen, 2010[4]; Pasnik & Llorente, 2012[5]).

Clearly, different technologies offer different potential for play and joint engagement. The previous section outlines the benefits of joint attention for peer-to-peer play and these are also important for parent-child engagement. When a parent and a child have a shared focus on educational content, e.g. a digital book or a children's programme they watch on the TV, they can better establish what is important and establish a connection between spoken words and words written or spoken on the screen. Such referencing is very important for the language development of young children.

With Apps for tablets and smartphones, parents can choose between those designed for children's independent or shared use. With the latter, parents can help children navigate the often complex world portrayed in specific applications. Advanced interactive Apps include animation, sound effects and personalisation features which allow the child to act as a direct participant in a story or game. Parents can also encourage children to create their own stories. Involving their family members is a great way of empowering young children in their digital skills, and these activities create a unique space for dialogue and co-learning. Parents can enrich children's stories by adding their own contents but also by guiding children's story-composing and writing. With iPad Apps, self-made stories are multimodal combinations of pictures, sounds and texts. Parents and children will have different levels of familiarity with each mode of story representation and so they can draw on each other's knowledge in putting together a story that recognises the multiple mode representation.

In one project carried out in England, a mother created a digital story together with her three-and-a-half-year old

Co-viewing

Research shows that when parents watch programmes with their children, the children tend to watch less TV, and they also gain more from the experience. The popular TV series Sesame Street and Joan Ganz Cooney Center in the US have been promoting the importance of co-viewing since early 1980s. Since then, it has been well-established that parents who watch TV jointly with their children can help them better understand the concepts portrayed on the screen and guide their attention to features salient for learning. The importance of joint media engagement applies to all media that children encounter at home.

daughter, based on the daily routines depicted by a toy clock. While the child was very skilled at audio-recording the narrative accompanying her story, she needed her mother's help with typing the words. In one of the exchanges, the child taught her mother how the App worked, while the mother showed her how to type some difficult words.

Child: Rosie? [The girl is typing random letters as part of her story]
Mother: No, t-t-t for tortoise. Here! [mother types T and adds it to child's writing]

When using technology together, parents and children can learn various digital literacy skills from each other; for example how to navigate some Apps, how to manipulate specific programmable toys or specific movements activating and controlling Wiis and other player movement games. Further to enjoying the world of technology-mediated play with their children, the parents' role is to choose the appropriate resource for their children and support them in using it effectively. Here are some tips to help you guide your choice:

● when to start and for how long to allow screen time,

● how to ensure safe play with technology, and

● how to choose the right resource.

How early and how much screen time should children be allowed

There is no official guidance on how often or how much children should be exposed to technology. So far the only available national guidance which contains age-specific restrictions is the American Paediatrics Association recommendation on screen use (see http://www.aap.org/en-us/advocacy-and-policy/aap-health-initiatives/Pages/Media-and-Children.aspx). This guiding document recommends no screen use (that is to say no computers, TV, tablets or smartphones) for children under the age of two years. It should be taken into account that the research this recommendation draws on is mostly TV. It also relies on the concern that thus far, there is little known about the effects of tablets or smartphones on infants' early language or socio-emotional development.

In interpreting this guidance parents should know that age guidelines vary by countries, with some professionals, for example German psychologists, recommending limited screen time for children under the age of six. Given that the research on the appropriateness of specific technologies for young developing brains is only emerging, it is necessary to use caution when it comes to the use of screens with very young children. What is clear is that a draconian rule about no screen time would be ill-advised given that today's children grow up surrounded by technology. While for very young children (under the age of two), screen-mediated experiences are not recommended, for older children it is more effective to educate them about appropriate use early on. It is also important to remember that each type of technology comes with a different set of benefits and challenges, and that parents need to evaluate them in terms of their value for a specific child, specific circumstances and context of their use.

How to ensure safe play with technology

Parents are crucial in facilitating children's safe play with technology, especially with Internet-enabled devices. If children have access to Internet-enabled computers or tablets at home, parents should know what sites their children visit, and how

they interact with them. As with any other resource, a site can be evaluated in terms of its learning and play potential, age appropriateness and suitability for a specific child. Parents can help children choose the appropriate website according to some simple rules of thumb and their own knowledge of the child's skills and preferences. In addition, it is the parents' role and responsibility that children's experiences with a particular website are not interrupted or disrupted with undesired web content. Parents might be well advised to adjust privacy settings, block certain services and enable safe search on the device that the child uses. They can also help children to identify sites where they can share their work and connect with friends in a safe way. Childnet International (http://www.childnet.com/parents-and-carers) works with thousands of parents and children aged 3-18. The charity documents children's experiences and shares a wealth of advice and tips on the safe and responsible use of online resources for young children. The Childnet International website contains detailed advice for parents wishing to find out more about how they can prevent cyberbulling and guard their children from sexting, grooming and pornography. Another important set of resources are available from KidSmart which includes a video and other support materials featuring 'Smartie Penguin' (see http://www.kidsmart.org.uk/teachers/ks1/watchsmartie.aspx).

Parents can also block or selectively enable tablet and smartphone Apps which contain in-App purchases and

Children's screen time

Like Apps, children's TV enables carers to leave children alone in the knowledge that they are being entertained. Children's programmes also make similar claims about supporting children's educational development. However, TV has been a part of our lives long enough for these claims to have been rigorously studied.

A large number of studies show potentially harmful effects of TV watching on young children's attention, learning, sleep and obesity. This has led the American Academy of Paediatrics to recommend zero hours of screen time for children aged zero to two years.

However, we need to differentiate between passive and active consumption of TV content and the context of watching. For instance, many of the claims about TV and links to obesity are not supported if we consider recent additions to TVs such as Wii, Xbox or LeapTV which offer more active ways of engaging with the content, often encouraging children to physically move as they watch. Active viewing and joint co-viewing of educational TV programme is also different from a child watching a film on their own.

premium rate content. These hidden costs may vary depending on resource and it is important that parents fully explore an App before they put it into a child's hands.

Good practice

Best practice examples are those where parents and children jointly interact with a piece of technology. Some technologies support this practice better than others. With open-ended story-making Apps (e.g. Our Story™, My Story™ and Story Maker™), children can audio-record, write short texts, take pictures or video how their parents teach them important life skills (e.g. a parent teaching their child to cook or explaining car maintenance to them). Involving other members of the family or community may enrich such a story with multigenerational 'funds of knowledge', as older members of the community may add a different perspective on the issue.

Co-creating stories

The Our Story™ App for tablets and smartphones enables parents and children to share their own stories in texts, pictures and sound. The App was designed for young children, with a clear user interface and simple navigation using large iconic buttons, with the aim of supporting parents and children in creating and sharing their own multimedia stories (see http://creet.open.ac.uk/

projects/our-story/). The user interface consists of a gallery of pictures and a storyboard, which resembles a filmstrip and is located at the bottom of the gallery of pictures. The storyboard (or 'filmstrip') enables users to put digital pictures into a sequence of book 'pages', and for each picture, users can add text and/or recorded sound. The App allows for open-ended multimedia content, that is, users can insert any pictures, texts or sounds they like to create their stories. The App is accessible as a free public download for both iOS and Android platforms from the Internet.

There are various ways in which the App could be used at home. For example, Andrea, mother of 33-month-old Lucy decided to create a multimodal story for her daughter, based on their recent holiday in the Mediterranean. Andrea inserted some pictures taken on holiday into the App and accompanied these with written captions and her own audio recordings describing what is happening in the individual pictures. Thus each picture contained a piece of text and audio-recording and contributed to the sequence of a multimedia story. Lucy has immediately taken to the story. When interacting with it together with her mother, Lucy sat on Andrea's lap, with the iPad in-between them. Lucy was swiping the pages to move from one page to another one and playing the sounds on individual pages. Andrea was supporting the experience by asking her daughter questions about what is happening in the picture and how that relates to Lucy's own memories from the holiday. There were times when they were both immersed in the imaginary story world, for example when talking about a doll called Suzanne:

Andrea: And what's Suzanne doing in this picture?

Lucy: Snoring! [child starts imitating snoring sound]

Andrea: [laughs] And what do we say to Suzanne when she's snoring?

Lucy: Wake up Suzanne, wake up!

In addition to encouraging free play and fantasy, Andrea also supported Lucy in narrating her own story. For instance she helped Lucy to recall how, where and when specific events occurred and used some pictures from the multimedia story to jog her memory.

Andrea: 'And here we are on a...? on a...slide. Do you remember?

Together, the mother and child had great fun not only sharing their experiences and memories of them but also jointly contributing to the multimedia story captured in a new format. The Our Story™ App can also serve as a good tool for recording family life.

Technology in the classroom

There are various ways in which teachers can promote play with technologies in their classrooms. A way of supporting imaginary play is to include ICT in book reading and storytelling sessions

All about...
ICT

With digital technology now an integral part of children's everyday lives, settings must consider how they can best use it to support learning. *Dr Christine Stephen* draws on 15 years of research to look at how children's preferences vary and what support educators can offer

Today's children are growing up in a century where digital technologies are commonplace for leisure, domestic life, work and study. Three- to five-year-olds are familiar with interactive television, DVDs, and using mobile phones to send messages, talk, play games and take photographs. They are likely to have played games on laptops or tablets, watched parents shop online and – although they are not able to read the results – pre-schoolers will suggest that parents or siblings 'Google it' when answers to their questions are not forthcoming. In shops and on outings, children watch their family using interactive devices to pay for purchases, obtain cash or services and get information.

The range of possible encounters with digital interactive and communicative technologies makes it clear that these resources are part of the environment that shapes the learning and development of young children. But while these technologies are commonplace, they are not welcome by everyone. There is an increasingly polarised debate about the advantages and disadvantages of children engaging with digital technologies in the pre-school years.

EDUCATORS' DILEMMA

Some argue that activities involving technologies are inappropriate for young children, encouraging passivity, social isolation and physical inactivity. On the other hand, engaging with technological resources can be seen as opening opportunities for acquiring knowledge and competencies, as necessary for children's future education and work in a knowledge economy, or simply as a fun way of ensuring or accelerating learning.

This debate is unlikely to be resolved soon, but the outcome is likely to be a more nuanced position that takes account of the context in which children are growing up and interacting with technologies. In the meantime, digital technologies are an inherent and ubiquitous part of children's everyday lives which respon-

Practitioners should consider if technologies offer different support for learning from more traditional activities

sive educators cannot ignore – just as they cannot ignore the impact of children's other activities at home. However, while there is plenty of writing about the potential of technology to support learning and development, there is less clear evidence about the impact of these new resources.

Current research suggests that while digital resources can enhance learning, much depends on the way in which educators make use of the technology and design features that support higher-order thinking. ➤

PHOTOS AT HAMPDEN WAY NURSERY SCHOOL BY JUSTIN THOMAS

Just as with traditional playroom activities, it seems that the efficacy of new technologies depends on the quality of the resource or activity and the pedagogic skills of educators who can identify and respond to the interests and needs of individual children in their setting.

LEARNING WITH NEW TECHNOLOGIES

It is useful to think of the kinds of outcomes that can be attributed to engaging with digital technologies in four categories.

Operational learning

Pre-school children do learn to use technological resources readily and with confidence and the touch-and-scroll interfaces offered by tablet computers and mobile phones are particularly advantageous for younger children. However, this kind of learning is not as 'instinctive' as the term 'digital natives' seems to imply when it is used to describe pre-schoolers. Children do get stuck and need help from more able others and that makes demands on the confidence with which educators use the digital resources in their playroom.

Knowledge of the world

This kind of learning comes as children use digital technologies to develop emerging skills and capacities, solve problems and test out answers.

We found examples of children developing their communication capacities as they made video recordings about life in their playroom. Life history projects were supported by reviewing digital photographs; listening to audio stories facilitated narrative skills and responding to music

clips extended children's descriptive vocabulary. Digital programmes provide opportunities to practise developing capacities such as counting, letter and sound recognition.

When playroom practices include supporting interest or project groups and children documenting their own learning, then digital technologies have much to offer, although children will still need the support of educators to read information, write questions or access files.

Family and peers

Technologically mediated leisure activities allow children to be active participants in family pursuits such as viewing films and music-making, planning outings and holidays.

In early years settings, encounters with technologies often involve participation with peers too, providing an arena where social roles and relationships are developed as children collaborate, compete and find ways to influence the activities of others.

POSITIVE DISPOSITIONS

The practitioners in our playroom studies provided clear evidence that as children engaged with new technologies they developed dispositions towards learning that are important in traditional and technological environments. They noticed children growing in confidence and self-esteem as they became more independent users of particular technologies and becoming more persistent when they encountered challenges with the resources.

Pre-school children have distinct likes and dislikes when it comes to digital technology

INDIVIDUAL PREFERENCES

In our studies of three- to five-year-olds, we found that children had a wide range of experiences with technologies at home. Some families were enthusiastic technology users, communicating with grandparents through Skype, downloading films and games and taking and reviewing digital photographs.

In a minority of homes, technologies were seen as only for adult use or as a feature of the work rather than the home environment and in these circumstances parents chose to postpone or limit their child's exposure to new technologies.

We found most parents were aware of the debate about the appropriate-

While digital resources can enhance learning, much depends on the way in which educators make use of the technology

ness of new technologies for young children and each family in our studies had set some limits on the length of time or circumstances in which their child could watch television or films or use the computer. Parents sought to balance time with technologies with physical activities such as swimming and playing in the garden.

Families and children differ along four dimensions that we found had an impact on the way any individual child engaged with technologies at home and in early years settings.

1. Perspective

Parents' perspectives on whether new technologies can help children learn influence the emphasis they give to purchasing resources and encouraging the use of technologies. One mother in our study was sceptical about the value of technologies for learning, preferring to buy flash cards rather than digital reading tools, but another parent was enthusiastic about the benefits her son gained from play with his toy laptop and games console and recommended them to others.

2. Supporting learning

Parents have different views on the most appropriate ways to support learning. Some children were encouraged to explore and find out for themselves what a resource could offer and their parents only helped when the youngsters were evidently frustrated. Other parents were more directive and concerned that children knew how to use the technologies properly.

3. Family practices and times

Family practices and the demands on parents' time make a difference. Children's access to technological resources is influenced by the needs of siblings and family priorities for leisure activities. Having older siblings usually meant that more sophisticated resources were available in the home, but the presence of younger siblings could mean access to technologies was limited to 'safe' times.

4. Individual preferences

Children's individual preferences were the most influential dimension. Pre-school children have distinct

👉

MORE INFORMATION

- 'Are we allowed to blink? Young children's leadership and ownership while mediating interactions around technologies' by L Arnott in *International Journal of Early Years Education*
- Briefings on digital childhoods, www. strath.ac.uk/ humanities/research/ digitalchildhoods
- *Growing up with technology: young children learning in a digital world* by L Plowman, C Stephen, and J McPake
- 'Seven myths about young children and technology' by L Plowman and J McPake in *Childhood Education*
- 'Young children engaging with technologies at home: the influence of family context' by C Stephen, O Stevenson and C Adey in *Journal of Early Childhood Research*

likes and dislikes when it comes to technologies, contrary to the widely held view among adults that all technologies are desirable to children.

The children in our studies ranged from enthusiastic game players who enjoyed competition to keen collectors of information about an enduring interest (for example, cars and trucks) and to others who had no sustainable interest in engaging with technology, even if they were growing up in a family where there was ample access to digital resources. The children were discriminating users of technologies; they identified games they liked and found fun and others that they found difficult or boring.

Children come to pre-school with a range of experiences with technological resources. Our evidence suggests that it is unlikely that interacting with technologies will dominate the lives of pre-school children, but they can be expected to have favourite digital and traditional activities.

Girls and boys often prefer different games or types of technologies, but gender alone does not predict interest in digital play. Some will be keen to explore the technology available in the playroom, others will expect to play competitive games and some will expect a more 'teacherly' introduction and seek a guide though the technologies available. And just as some prefer outdoor play or construction or painting, children will differ in their willingness to engage with whatever technologies are available in the playroom.

TECHNOLOGIES IN EARLY YEARS SETTINGS
Selecting resources

Educators will want to consider the extent to which digital resources in the playroom replicate children's experiences at home (where they often have access to more up-to- ➤

Careful attention must be given to the choice of resources and how children can access them

date resources) and if they offer different support for learning from traditional activities. It is important that practitioners consider if computer programs and games are founded on the same understanding about how to nurture learning as that on which they base their own practice.

Many programs targeted at pre-school children use closed questions rather than prompts for exploration and give the answer after a set number of incorrect responses, which does little to help children understand how to arrive at the correct answer.

Although adults tend to refer to children's engagement with technologies as play, not all are experienced as playful by the children and playroom rules can further constrain the spontaneous and creative aspects of playful behaviour. Many art or drawing packages are nearer to traditional 'colouring in' than opportunities for self-expression, but making videos or animated films can foster creative activity as well as problem solving and developing group work skills.

The responsive educator
Perhaps even more important than ensuring that the resources match the pedagogic intentions of educators is the finding that children need adults to support their engagement with technologies. Children do experience difficulties with digital technologies and we observed youngsters giving up and turning to other activities, a response that is often masked by the ready availability of other options in early years settings.

Although adults often claim that children are more competent technology users than they are themselves, research evidence makes it clear that if children's interactions with digital resources are to be the kind of intense

and sustained encounters that are associated with positive learning experiences, then support from responsive others is essential. Technology does not remove or reduce the role of the educator. Our studies found that two types of support from educators (and parents) are needed – distal and proximal guided interaction.

Distal guided interaction
Distal guided interaction is the kind of thinking and activity that educators do when children are not present. It refers to:
- planning next steps in learning
- choosing resources and activities reflecting children's interests or the focus of their current explorations
- decisions about what resources to buy, where to locate them and how to monitor children's progress.

Educators need to ensure equitable access to the digital resources, toys and games provided and consider how to deploy staff so that an adult

Many programs use closed questions rather than prompts for exploration

can be available to interact with children as they use technologies.

Of course, none of these kinds of decisions are new to educators; they are part of everyday pedagogic planning. Nevertheless, it is important to point out that children's positive interactions with technologies require the same kind of careful attention to the role of educator as any other activity.

Proximal guided interaction
Young children need proximal guided interaction too – the face-to-face interactions with adults who can model how to use resources, demonstrate, explain, and ask what would happen if alternatives were tried. Sometimes children need physical guidance such as an adult hand over their hand on a control, while at other times what is needed is help to negotiate the social context that surrounds the digital play.

Pre-schoolers need emotional support too: support when listening to an audio recording gets too scary, praise for achievements, someone to share the fun of an animation or pleasure in a new discovery. Adults are needed to read instructions, scaffold the search for information, prompt sorting and categorising, interpret feedback and scores and recognise when a child needs to develop an understanding of a new concept in a more concrete or active way before practising this new knowledge with a computer program.

CONCLUSION
Digital technologies are part of the everyday lives of three- to five-year-olds, and early years educators will want to build on that aspect, just as they do with other home experiences. Finding out about children's preferences among technological and traditional activities is an important part of home-school communication.

Responsive planning and skilful interactions with educators are necessary if the opportunities which new technologies offer – to extend children's learning and provide engaging ways of practising new skills and interacting with peers – are to be realised. ■

Dr Christine Stephen, a research fellow at the School of Education, University of Stirling, focuses on children's learning experiences. Here, she draws on findings from a series of externally funded studies that she has carried out over a period of 15 years with colleagues Lydia Plowman and Joanna McPake with children. Several schools run regular interactive whiteboard (IW) stories or individual and group reading sessions with digital books. While most teachers would be familiar with e-books which can be displayed on the interactive whiteboard, not so many use book-making Apps to support children's imagination and creativity, as well as literacy skills. With book-making software and tablet Apps, teachers can create their own digital books together with the child. They can do so using various templates provided by the book-making software or by creating their own templates which are aligned with their pedagogical objectives. The more open-ended the book-making program is, the more possibilities teachers have to customise the session according to their preferences. For example, with the RealeWriter™ software, children and adults can create any audio-visual book which can be printed or shared as a multimodal file via email. The software is available for free in its Pro version from: http://realewriter.com/

Story-making Apps designed for tablets and young children, e.g. StoryMaker™, My Story™ and Our Story™ have similar functionalities- children can add their own texts, audio-recordings and pictures directly taken with the tablet camera. The finished stories can be printed out or shared via email/ dropbox. With the Our Story™ App, users can choose from various print formats, including A4 or A5.

Furthermore, teachers have used the Our Story™ App for a number of different storytelling activities. For example, Daniella decided to use the Our Story™ App to enable children in her classroom to add story extensions to the popular Spot the Dog! Story[6]. There were various stages to the activity: At the beginning of the session, Daniella used a laptop and the PowerPoint programme to display the electronic version of the book on the interactive whiteboard. She wanted to make sure that all the children in the class understood what the story was about and what their task will be. To do so, she read the book on the IW page by page, and selectively chose children to help with the reading. Children quickly realised that the book displayed on the IW had been modified by their teacher: instead of the dog hiding in the book, their teacher had replaced visuals of Spot with the faces of each of the children in the class. Children loved the idea and were keen to personalise their own versions of the story as a small group activity. The next step was then to add their own captions and pictures to books, based on the 'Spot the Dog' theme.

To do so, children needed to decide which picture to use from an array of pictures available on the iPad. Once the children identified the picture that they would like to use, the second task was to annotate it with text or add an audio-recording or a combination of both. Thirdly, the finished picture needed to be placed in the filmstrip at the bottom of the screen. This enabled the children to see the sequence of their story as it emerged, and make informed decisions as to which picture they should choose next to continue their tale.

In another classroom, through a collaboration project initiated by The University of Nottingham and led by Prof Colin Harrison, an

English and an American primary school exchanged ideas and friendship through RealeBooks, i.e. digital books created with the RealeWriter™ software[7]. The two schools, one in Nottingham, England, and one in Austin, Texas, have exchanged 'innovation challenges' and strategies to develop creative problem-solving which have been captured in their digital books. The children began by thinking up inventions that would improve their own school environment, such as a new kind of bird table that would discourage large birds from taking all the bird food, or an electronic tagging system for finding lost pencils at the end of a lesson. Gradually the children's ideas became more creative and inventive, and included an electronic lead to enable small girls to walk large dogs, and 'sister-cancelling headphones' that enabled the wearer (an older brother) to mask the speech of his younger sister with white noise!

These examples show that with open-ended story-making technologies, children can produce and publish writing, collaborate with others and even jointly solve problems. If children cannot yet write, they can compose their stories by assembling the story characters and audio-record their stories. They can also add drawings to their stories or annotate pictures, for example the 30Hands™ App provides great flexibility in terms of adding and editing children's own content in a variety of formats.

Another great activity to try out in the classroom is to encourage the creation of multilingual versions of a story. With story-making

Apps, children can easily record their own voice-overs in various languages and thus diversify the story resources available in the classroom. A teacher can, for example, provide some pictures as a template in a digital story (easily done with the Our Story™ App or the RealeWriter™ software) and let children annotate these with their own captions or recordings in their native languages. With the Me Books™ App, children and adults can record their own sounds and add these to the digital stories.

Children's play with ICT does not need to solely rely on technology. It is also good to think about whether ICT enriches the off screen version of an activity. For example, if a reading App links to audio books, such as through a QR code, children can make connections between various resources. Also, Apps might be used to teach children specific concepts (for example the principle of balance) and then encourage children to walk the balance beam outside. ICT can also add great fun to dancing and singing activities, for instance children can record their own voices or video their dance performances and share their creations with their friends or parents at home. Apps can also be used to hone specific skills that children may use to enrich their creative play. For instance, with the Peg&Cat Big™ App, they can explore their musical imaginations as they can pick up an instrument and pretend to play it. With the Toca Band™ App, children can play and creatively experiment with rhythms and sounds beats. As children create their own

musical pieces, encourage them to dance along, either as individuals or groups – this can be great fun!

Remember that the best uses of ICT are those that extend and enrich off screen activities- not replace them. Adults- whether parents, teachers or other primary caregivers- are crucial in supporting children's engagement with technology and if possible, should always explore technology-mediated play together with their children.

References

1. Seitz, V., Rosenbaum, L.K., & Apfel, N.H. (1985). Effects of family support intervention: A ten-year follow-up. *Child Development*, 56(2), 376-391.

2. Melhuish, E.C., Sylva, K., Sammons, P., Siraj-Blatchford, I., & Taggart, B. (2001). *The Effective Provision of Pre-school Education Project, Technical Paper 7: Social/Behavioural and Cognitive Development at 3-4 Years in Relation to Family Background*. London: Institute of Education/DfES.

3. Rice, M.L., Huston, A.C., Truglio, R., & Wright, J.C. (1990). Words from "Sesame Street": Learning vocabulary while viewing. *Developmental Psychology*, 26(3), 421.

4. Plowman, L., McPake, J., & Stephen, C. (2010). The technologisation of childhood? Young children and technology in the home. *Children & Society*, 24(1), 63–74.

5. Pasnik, S., & Llorente, C. (2012). *Study of Preschool Parents and Caregivers Use of Technology and PBS KIDS Transmedia Resources: A Report to the CPB-PBS "Ready to Learn Initiative"*. Boston: Education Development Center, Inc.

6. Kucirkova, N., Willans, D., & Cremin, T. (2014) *Spot the dog!* Spot the difference, English 4-11, Summer edition, 11-14.

7. Harrison, C. & Kucirkova, N. (2011) *RealeBooks: let your students design and publish their own books!* Deutsch Differenziert, October, Vol4, pp. 39-44.

ICT across the curriculum

This book has been written for an international readership at the end of the first UN Decade of Education for Sustainable Development (2005-14), which has aimed to accelerate the implementation of a new vision in education. It is also a year in which the UN will launch Sustainable Development Goals, that take the place of the international Millennium Development Goals that set targets for addressing global poverty, exclusion and promoted gender equality, education, and environmental sustainability. In the circumstances, a section on ESD might be considered justified in those terms alone.

Outdoor education and ICT

A false dichotomy is drawn between ICT and outdoor and environmental education in early childhood. This is extremely misleading and we feel that the evidence really needs to be presented. Both parents and professionals have expressed concerns about the time children spend in front of a screen. In recent years, greater emphasis has rightly been placed on the importance of the outdoor learning environment for young children, and this is sometimes presented as compensation for 'toxic' influences upon early childhood that include ICT (Palmer, 2007)[1]. Yet many other parents, professionals and pre-schools are demonstrating through their practice that this is in fact a false dichotomy (Egbert, 2015)[2]. They are showing how ICT can be integrated across the curriculum to support children's development in a broad and balanced manner. Exercise is important in early childhood and children need the space and encouragement to engage in vigorous physical activity. Where excessive sedentary behaviour is identified, whether it be in front of a television or computer screen, engaging in too much formal literacy or numeracy activities, colouring in, or any other activity, children should be encouraged to be more physically active. Research suggests that the main barriers to physically active play in early childhood are related to the physical layout of pre-schools, the provision of outdoor play areas, and the opportunities made available to use them. While a positive ethos of adult encouragement, and the availability of specific outdoor equipment and activities are important, the most important thing is access (Brady et al., 2008)[3]. By logical extension, this applies equally to the children's time away from pre-school and to the home learning environment. Children need space and the freedom to physically engage in active play every day. When that is available, children are generally motivated to use it.

The fact is that however anxious some early childhood educators are regarding ICTs, ICTs play a significant role in children's lives and in the lives of their families, and should therefore feature just as strongly in the curriculum as any other aspect of environmental education.

It has even been suggested at times that ICT and outdoor play might in some fundamental sense be logically inconsistent. Yet such a case could only really be argued if one were to first assume that all ICTs were associated with desktop computers. This is demonstrably not the case. As adults we interact with a wide range of ICTs outdoors, and many of these may be applied for educational purposes. Laptop computers, smart phones and tablets all have rechargeable batteries, and many have wireless Wi-Fi and/or 3/4G Internet connections. Cameras, metal detectors, traffic lights, robotic and radio controlled vehicles, Global Positioning System (GPS) and a wide range of other Apps accessed through mobile telephones and tablets provide additional examples of ICTs that have been applied effectively in and around a wide range of pre-school settings.

There is undoubtedly a good deal of scope for the integration of ICT in young children's outdoor play environments. In fact, ICT is as much a part of a child's world (indoors and outdoors) as literacy and numeracy, or indeed any other feature of the complex worlds in which we live and struggle to make sense of. This is recognised at Reggio Emilia, one of the most celebrated models of pre-school practice in the world. At Reggio Emilia the pre-school classrooms have an atelier, a room where children can find all the tools an artist might need: paints, paper, pens, clay, wire, a camera as well as a computer, printer, scanner, video monitors. There are also video projectors in many of the ateliers and the children are taught how to use the equipment to produce images on paper and images, transformations, animations, and video clips (Edwards et al., 2012)[4].

Education for sustainable development

It is also now widely accepted that a key objective for outdoor education is to contribute towards Education for Sustainable Development (ESD) which may be thought of: "[...]

as a process of learning how to make decisions that take into consideration the long-term future of the economy, ecology and equity of communities" (United Nations Educational, Scientific and Cultural Organisation, UNESCO, 2013)[5]. ICT has an established role in providing ESD at all levels in education, and the UNESCO established a University Chair in Information and Communication Technologies (ICTs) in Education for Sustainable Development (ESD) in 2008. Increasing global access to education is itself an objective of ESD, and ICT is already contributing significantly in this respect both formally and informally, as Internet access broadens the opportunities for people to obtain information, to interact and to create support networks. In India for example, despite relatively low levels of access to the Internet from computers, more than 240 million already access some form of Internet services on their mobiles.

Africa has the highest Mobile Learning growth rate in the world. The five-year compound annual growth rate (CAGR) for the Mobile Learning market in Africa is 38.9%. Revenues will grow more than five times to reach $530.1 million by 2017, up from the $102.4 million reached in 2012 (Adkins, 2015)[6]. The UNESCO recently completed a survey on mobile reading in seven developing countries, and the study reported that hundreds of thousands of people are already reading full-length books on mobile phones, even phones with small black and white screens. The key findings of the study include:

- Mobile reading opens up new pathways to literacy for marginalised groups, particularly women and girls, and others who may not have access to paper books.

- People use mobile devices to read to children, thereby supporting literacy acquisition and other forms of learning.

- People seem to enjoy reading more and read more often when they use mobile devices to access text.

- Most mobile readers are young, yet people of various ages are capable of using mobile technology to access long-form reading material. More can be done to encourage older people to use technology to access texts and literature.

- There appears to be a demand for mobile reading platforms with text in local languages, level-appropriate text and text written by local authors (UNESCO, 2014).[7]

Paas (2008)[8] argued that ICTs play an important role in advancing ESD in two ways:

- by increasing access to educational materials about sustainability (e.g. via distance learning, educational networks and databases), and

- by helping to promote new ways of interacting in order to facilitate the learning called for in ESD, that emphasises not just knowledge, but choices, values and actions.

Good practice

ICT provides online tools that can be used to measure both school and home 'carbon footprints' (see http://www.carbonfootprint.com/calculator.aspx). It also provides the tools to support us in building a more just, equal, human and environmentally-friendly world. ICT can contribute to early childhood ESD through the use of:

- learning from a wide range of computer programs, Apps, video and animations,

- simulation games, and

- (adults) supporting children's Internet search, e.g. contributing to investigative project work.

ESD educational games include the iOS Apps, e.g. Gro Garden™, Gro Recycling™ and Toca Nature™. Apps are subtle and may require initial adult encouragement, but Toca Nature™ has a lot to offer. It enables children to:

- plant trees, create lakes, and build mountains,

- collect berries, nuts, and mushrooms,

- feed animals, and

- explore the forest.

Free educational iOS Apps for early childhood also include Get Water™ and Zoe makes a splash!™, a multilingual App developed by the European Union. There are many e-storybook Apps with environmental protection themes; these include the free Green Rank– Save our Oceans™, which is all about keeping the oceans clean and why that is important; RecyClaire™ and Gimme Gimme™. Another example is the relatively expensive but charming, The Lorax™, a Dr. Seuss e-storybook App which supports learning about the importance of taking care of our environment and trees. Children can help the Lorax regrow the world's Truffula tree forests! ESD related online activities that may be suitable with adult support include:

- Kids at National Geographic: http://kids.nationalgeographic.com/

Adults may also find some good games at: http://ecogamer.org/environmental-games.

Some Apps are better for classroom group activities than others. Green Up™ is a US (iPad/iPhone/iPod touch) App that supports interaction and decision-making. As the above reference to Paas (2008)[8] suggested, learning about sustainability is not sufficient. Children need to learn to develop relevant values and learn to make better choices and actions. Children will not learn to participate actively in society if they are not helped to become aware of the problems and challenges that we face, and (crucially) their own capability in contributing to solving them (Freire, 1977)[9]. Increasingly,

ICTs applications are being designed to promote collaboration, connectivity, 'real-world', experience-based learning, and systems thinking, which are emerging as key pedagogical methods conducive to educating for sustainability. (Ekendra, 2013)[10]

Young children benefit from open-ended discussions, and meaningful medium or long-term 'project' or 'topic' or investigation based activities (Helm & Katz, 2001)[11]. Curriculum integration works well in the early years, and language, science, design and technology, social studies, dramatic play, and artistic creation may all be usefully brought together to create meaningful activities that are relevant to the child's life experiences and in supporting ESD. Project work is led by a theme, which integrates the curriculum for the child. As Katz and Chard (2000, p.10)[12] have argued, even in the pre-school:

[...] project work can strengthen children's dispositions to be empirical, that is, to seek and to examine available evidence and facts, to check their predictions and hypotheses, and to learn to be open to alternative ways of interpreting facts and findings. In addition, project work provides opportunities to strengthen their disposition to work hard, presents occasions of having to do some things over again to meet the participants' developing standards, and to find satisfaction in overcoming obstacles and difficulties.

One of the most celebrated models of Early Childhood education (Reggio Emilia) very explicitly adopts this approach. They:

- encourage analysis, synthesis and evaluation,

- encourage the children to share their knowledge and ideas,

- encourage integrated project work, and

- be a 'partner' in the activity (Edwards & Hiler, 1993)[13].

As Edwards and Hiler (1993)[13] suggested,

Young children are already developmentally capable of high level thinking skills, including analysis (e.g. seeing similarities and differences); synthesis (e.g. rearranging, reorganizing); and evaluation (judging the value of materials). We should encourage them to practice these skills.

One of the most significant contributions that can be made to this by technology is also a priority in Reggio Emilia. It is to

'document' the children's learning, e.g. recording their activity through photographs, videos, printouts, and screen captured images, etc. These:

- provide evidence of children's learning,

- provide context for parent partnership, and

- provide an ongoing means of monitoring progress.

Young children can express their ideas in a variety of ways using a variety of symbolic media. When we encourage them to share their experiences and learn from others, they can also develop their expressive repertoire even further. This:

- strengthens the child's disposition to learn,

- makes the learning more meaningful and relevant,

- provides motivation for emergent literacy,

- supports long-term social and emotional development, and

- is more engaging for children and parents.

One example of this kind of activity is featured in a pre-school training video (Abbott et al., 1996)[14], that involved a group of

children embarking on a 'ladybird hunt'. The case provides a good example of the project/investigative approach that Siraj-Blatchford and MacLeod-Brudenell (1999)[15] referred to as playing the 'game' of being a scientist. A number of the activities within the pre-school had been related to the topic of 'living things and patterns in nature'. One of the children observed a ladybird in a raised flower bed during outdoor play, and an adult took this opportunity to spend a few minutes showing the children some reference books that featured ladybirds.

The video is a few years old and today it is more likely that she would have 'googled' the information. As she talked to the children she seemed genuinely curious about the insects and she encouraged the children to take an interest as well.

They looked at the pictures and they talked about the ladybird's spots, its wings and wing covers. They also talked about how they should always take care of living things. One of the children asked where ladybirds lived and what it was that they ate, so they decided to investigate and see if they could find some that could be captured in 'pooters' and brought into the setting:

> *There was an air of anticipation and excitement before they embarked outside [...] The children looked at the ladybirds through their magnifying glasses. They counted their spots with the help of the adult and they allowed them to crawl across their hands, and watched them fly. The children were then given the opportunity to make their own model ladybirds out of red and black playdough. (Siraj-Blatchford & MacLeod-Brudenell, 1999, p.10)[15]*

In another, more recent extended project, focused on Bat conservation in a Dorset pre-school, a wide range of technology was applied. The children learnt about the importance of the world's forests, the threats to their existence and the heroic work of people like the Nobel Prize winning Kenyan, Wangari Maathai in protecting them. The children were given practical activities identifying all the things around them that are made from wood/card/paper etc. A YouTube video provided a motivating video featuring Wangari Maathai telling a story about a little hummingbird whose behaviour in trying to save a forest was questioned by other animals (see https://www.youtube.com/watch?v=IGMW6YWjMxw). The hummingbird responded by constantly telling them: 'I'm just doing the best I can'.

Throughout the project, the children's attention was constantly drawn to the fact that the animals, plants, trees and people who work in the forest can only make things happen (or grow) very slowly 'a little bit at a time' and that they could only do the 'best they can'. The phrase 'I'm doing the best I can' was often repeated throughout the project. The children made model bats to play with, and they finally installed a conservation 'bat box' on a tree in the pre-school grounds. Information was accessed on the internet, video and still photographs were used to document the project activities, and it was reported to parents using a blog. One evening, parents came back to the pre-school with the

children and siblings to see the bats in flight, hunting moths and other insects, and a local volunteer brought in some electronic 'Heterodyne' bat detector units which helped to identify the bats and added significantly to the experience.

References

1   Palmer, S. (2007). *Toxic Childhood: How the Modern World is Damaging Our Children and What We Can Do about It.* Hachette: Orion Publishing.

2   Egbert, M. (2015). *Why my kids never experience nature. HIPMOMBRARIAN: Saving the World One Book at a Time.* Available at: http://hipmombrarian.com/2014/03/15/why-my-kids-never-experience-nature/

3   Brady, L, Gibb, J., Henshall, A., & Lewis, J. (2008). *Play and Exercise in Early Years: Physical Active Play in Early Childhood Provision.* London: Department for Culture, Media and Sport. Available at: http://dera.ioe.ac.uk/10527/1/Playresearch2008.pdf

4   Edwards, C., L. Gandini, & G. Forman (Eds.) (2012). *The Hundred Languages of Children: The Reggio Emilia Approach in Transformation.* (3rd ed.) Santa Barbara, CA: Praeger.

5   United Nations Educational, Scientific and Cultural Organisation (UNESCO) (2013). *Education for Sustainable Development (ESD) in the UK – Current Status, Best Practice and Opportunities for the Future.* London: National Commission for UNESCO.

6   Adkins, S. (2015). *Africa mobile learning market surges to $530.1 million by 2017.* Ambient Insight Research. Available at: http://www.ambientinsight.com/News/Ambient-Insight-2012-2017-Africa-Mobile-Learning-Market.aspx

7   United Nations Educational, Scientific and Cultural Organisation (UNESCO) (2014). *Reading in the Mobile Era: A Study of Mobile Reading in Developing Countries.* Paris: UNESCO.

8   Paas, L. (2008). *How Information and Communications Technologies Can Support Education for Sustainable Development: Current Uses and Trends.* Manmitoba, Canada: International Institute for Sustainable Development.

9   Freire, P. (1977). I *Agogi tou Katapiezomenou [The Education of the Oppressed].* Athens: Rappas.

10 Ekendra (2013). *Better education via effective information & communications technologies for sustainable development – ICT4Education.* Available at: http://ict4d.co/research/better-education-via-effective-information-communications-technologies-for-sustainable-development-ict4education/

11 Helm, J., & Katz, L. (2001). *Young Investigators: The Project Approach in the Early Years.* New York: Teachers College Press.

12 Katz, L., & Chard, S.C. (2000). *Engaging Children's Minds: The Project Approach.* Stamford, CT: Ablex Publishing Corporation.

13 Edwards, C.P., & Hiler, C. (1993). *A Teacher's Guide to the Exhibit: The Hundred Languages of Children.* Lexington, KY: College of Human Environmental Sciences, University of Kentucky.

14 Abbott, L., Marsh, C., & Griffin, B. (1996). *Firm Foundations: Quality Education in the Early Years. A Video Resource Pack.* Manchester: The Manchester Metropolitan University.

15 Siraj-Blatchford, J., & MacLeod-Brudenell, I. (1999). *Supporting Science, Design and Technology in the Early Years.* Buckingham: Open University Press.

Best practice guidance and e-safety

Guidance for pre-schools

Many examples of activities that may be developed for use in pre-schools have been provided in this book. These include the encouragement of socio-dramatic and imaginary play through including real or toy/pretend ICTs in children's play environments. Both still and video cameras have numerous applications including their use in the development of audio-visual books and story-making Apps.

In some homes and pre-schools, parents and professional educators have extended their partnership from established 'shared reading' practices to encourage playful learning with handheld devices or at the computer screen. But in many there is important work to be done. Communication between professional educators and parents is really important in the early years, and a better connection between the aims of parents and staff can lead to better outcomes for the children (Morgan & Siraj-Blatchford, 2013)[1]. Pre-school staff have found many ways that ICTs can be applied to support parents by:

● Using digital, still and video pictures in the entrance lobby, providing a record of trips, a typical day's activities, curriculum presentations, and special events,

● using digital pictures in children's records of achievement,

● sharing and asking parents to try out new software and Apps at home,

● using closed circuit TV to enable parents to watch children at play and learning (this can be improvised cheaply with a security camera),

- lending ICT hardware (e.g. camera, laptop and tablet, etc.) to parents for use at home,

- recording children singing and providing CDs/downloads, etc., and

- the development of websites, blogs and Facebook pages, etc.

(Adapted from: Morgan & Siraj-Blatchford, 2013)[1].

Home learning differs from school learning and teachers can easily underestimate the knowledge that children bring with them from home. Often, expectations made of children in the early years are too low, with teachers often providing less demanding activities than those experienced by children in stimulating home environments. But some parents may not be aware of the need to provide their children with this kind of stimulation, and they may also introduce their children to activities that are developmentally inappropriate. Therefore the teacher has an important role in explaining the rationale of the learning activities to be promoted in both the home and the pre-school. Perhaps the most common misunderstandings are related to the nature and function of 'play' and those related to the 'emergent' literacy and numeracy activities (e.g. 'mark making') that are encouraged prior to more formal instruction in reading, writing and arithmetic. A booklet or parent guide and FAQs on the school website can explain the value of these practices clearly and succinctly. But it is important not to rely on technology alone for this. Technology cannot be a substitute for pre-school staff in providing a warm, caring and welcoming environment for parents and other primary carers, or in showing an ongoing willingness to discuss the learning activities that are provided, and a child's progress with these activities.

It is important that practitioners feel confident in explaining the significance of children's early play to parents. They need to be clear in their own minds that play is not offered as an alternative to education, but that it provides the most effective means of ensuring the child's long-term educational success. Robust research has suggested that ICT can provide good contexts for playful exploration and educational value for pre-school children. Adults can usefully interact with children in their play with ICTs. Adult intervention provides scaffolding and an opportunity for the input of new skills or knowledge to enable the play to continue to develop (Wood & Attfield, 2005)[2]. Adults must recognise that play is educationally valuable, and that they should interact with children in their play and 'extend' the play, rather than dominating or directing it away from the child's intentions (Tamburrini, 1982)[3]. It is the teachers who must take the lead responsibility in developing partnerships with parents and library staff, as they are the ones with the expert knowledge and the professional role to do so. Pre-school staff can work towards a closer partnership by creating an ethos of belonging to the setting. This ethos can be characterised by:

- encouraging visits to the pre-school classroom,

- regular and effective communications,

- sharing responsibility and a willingness to work together,

e-safety

Serious concerns have been voiced about the extended periods of time spent by some young children in passive viewing of screen content. Some of the research that has been carried out to evaluate the effects of passive television viewing is worrying. The American Academy of Paediatrics recommends that children of pre-school age have less than one screen hour per day, and this should include all ICTs, including television and video. In Australia, the Royal Children's Hospital in Melbourne refers specifically to particular problems associated with the excessive television viewing upon children under two years of age. In the UK, it has been suggested that sedentary (e.g. television or desktop) screen viewing might reasonably be limited to no more than 10 to 20 minutes for three year olds, extending to no more than 40 minutes by the age of eight. Although the guidance that was originally developed in relation to the European Developmentally Appropriate Technology in Early Childhood (DATEC) project goes on to qualify this by arguing: "...if a child or group of children is totally engaged in an activity and the completion of this requires a longer period at the computer this should be allowed, but it would not be desirable to encourage children to do this regularly". (Siraj-Blatchford and Siraj-Blatchford, 2002)[4]. Crucially all of this guidance refers to passive viewing time and in these pages our emphasis has been upon screen time that is far from passive, screen time that is enriched by interaction with adults and peers, and that encourages off screen activity. As the US National Association for the Education of Young Children (NAEYC, 2012)[5], has concluded:

"The amount of time children spend with technology and media is important but how children spend time with technology must also be taken into account when determining what is effective and appropriate" (p3).

Many of the best apps and software applications currently available for this age group operate off line. But if pre-schools give children access to the internet or to app download services they should adjust privacy settings, block inappropriate sites and services, and enable safe search on any device that young children are given access to. Where greater freedoms are provided, the best advice currently available on cyberbullying, sexting, grooming and pornography should be consulted and followed (see Choosing the right resoures section).

- being approachable and respectful,

- taking time to explain and listen carefully,

- a willingness to share information and planning, and

- a willingness to ask parents for advice about their child.

Development through play

The ways in which children progress through play have been subject to extended research. We know that play begins with solitary play and that the child goes on to develop the capability to share, then to co-operate, and finally to collaborate in their play. Children's play develops as they develop and learn, so that the play of a three year old is quite different from that of a five year old. Siraj-Blatchford (2007)[6] identified the major features of progression in play as:

- infants and young children use symbols or signs in their emotional communications,

- they begin using symbols and signs in pretend play,

- pretend role play and object substitution become internalised as imagination,

- play has a fundamental influence in cognitive development, at first as they 'pretend', and then become more capable pretenders,

- socio-dramatic play becomes more collaborative as partners at first share symbols and then reciprocally negotiate roles,

- conceptual knowledge and understanding of the 'other', and of the 'self', develop further and learning 'dispositions' become more significant, and

- most children become oriented towards more formal learning and school subjects and disciplines (communities of practice).

ICT resources have been identified to support socio-dramatic role play and imaginary play. Pre-school staff can apply ICT in emergent literacy and numeracy activities including digital book reading and storytelling sessions with children. Teachers need to plan and organise integrated offline/off screen activities for the children. By the time they are four years old, most children can be supported in the use of book-making Apps to compose stories and narrative reports. Teachers can also use these tools to provide multilingual resources. Effective practitioners:

- talk with the children to give new meanings to objects and actions, treating them as symbols for other things,

- talk with the children about their actions and about objects to remind them of past experiences,

- encourage the children to use their imagination in developing their role-play with other children,

- improvise with all the available resources to create props to support role-play, and

- engage with and join in (when appropriate) the children's imaginative role-play.

Practitioners must listen carefully to what children say and take full account of what they say in their responses. While practitioners should avoid asserting their own direction to the children's play, they should provide prompts to stimulate the children's thinking, and also provide appropriate materials (including ICTs) to extend children's thinking, encouraging them to make connections between different activities, materials and contexts.

Guidance for parents and carers

Parents are critically important when it comes to technology and very young children. They are the ones who support children's

playful learning at home, choose activities and resources and coordinate the length and frequency of their use.

When it comes to technology, parents need to grapple with some important questions, for example when is the appropriate age to introduce technology to children and how to best use it to support specific skills. In her book *Screen Time How Electronic Media – From Baby Videos to Educational Software – Affects Your Young Child*, education journalist Lisa Guernsey[7] summarised the importance of taking into account three Cs: the Context and the Content of a specific piece of technology and how the two dovetail with the needs of a particular Child. These three Cs are crucial for understanding the learning potential of any technology, digital and non-digital. The three Cs principle is followed in numerous reports concerned with technology and early years education, including the "T" Is for Technology" report by RAND http://www.rand.org/education/projects/t-is-for-technology.html), a useful resource for any parents looking for straightforward answers to the main questions about technology use with young children.

What can parents do to support their children's responsible and effective use of technology? Here are some quick tips:

● Keep TVs, tablets and other large screens out of children's bedrooms. For young children, do not allow unsupervised use of Wi-Fi or 3/4G enabled technology.

● Make sure that your child is safe when using the Internet, whether they uses smart phones, tablets, laptops or games consoles. Use filters for websites which are popular with young children but which often contain inappropriate content, for example YouTube videos.

● Check the age appropriateness of devices as well as software programmes and their benefits for your child. However, note that the developer's guidance may often be misleading. It is best to check various sources and rely on your own knowledge of your child's needs.

● Act as a model to children as they learn to use these devices in social situations. If your children see you using your mobile phone while talking with them at the dinner table, they are likely to adopt the same behaviour when they grow up. Balance your media usage and do not allow smartphones and tablets to take over precious face-to-face time.

● Teach your child to be actively involved in the creation, not only consumption of digital content. Coding and computational thinking have become part of the national curriculum in several schools worldwide. The more you can discuss and experience with your child coding, the better they are prepared for a successful future in the world they grow up into.

● Set family guidelines that you will all agree to on online use and screen time. The rules will work best if they are developed together with the children. For example, ask your child how much and when they would like to use screen time for learning (e.g. accessing new information) and how much and when for socialising (e.g. for communicating with friends via Facebook). Teach them the various roles that technology can play in their lives and the value of time spent on various activities online and off screen.

● Be involved in your child's use of digital media as much as possible. Children learn more with adult instruction, so do join them as they explore the world of Minecraft (https://minecraft.net/) or explore various websites together with them. The more you are involved in these activities, the more you can be part of the digital world together with your child, and thus better understand the benefits and challenges it offers.

Guidance for library service providers

Whilst ICT ownership, access and use with young children are rapidly increasing, debates on the effects of ICT usage on children's learning and development continue. Therefore practitioners and caregivers can sometimes feel confused and helpless. However, it is essential that they are aware of the potential risks of misusing ICT and that they learn how to make the most of the available ICT to support children's early learning. In this respect, library service providers could help by offering constructive recommendations on how to carefully select, critically evaluate and effectively use ICT with/ for children.

What can library service providers do to support families with children in effective use of ICT?

Here are some quick tips:

- Provide equal access to new technologies for young children in the library. In accordance with the suggested screen time, the loan period should be restricted to one to two hours. Adults' presence is necessary in order to avoid children's passive and inappropriate use of the technology content.

- Integrate ICT into early literacy programmes (e.g. storytelling sessions) in the library. Remember that activities can be enriched with ICT, but should not be ICT-driven. Also, the focus should be on promoting parent-child or peer-to-peer activities, where people can learn from observing, remembering and imitating each other. A large screen is necessary for demonstration, and it is important to leave enough time for activity planning, design, implementation and evaluation.

- Link the library's early literacy programmes to pre-school curricula, in order to support the home-school connection. Deliver ICT training for practitioners and caregivers, e.g. parents, babysitters and pre-school teachers. This can provide practitioners and caregivers with relevant knowledge and skills, and would ultimately be of particular value to disadvantaged children.

- Provide children with developmentally appropriate ICT resources, services and programmes. Apps pre-downloaded in the library's tablets and used in library programmes indicate the library's tacit endorsement of the App's educational value, which would be important to practitioners and caregivers.

- Encourage library service providers to receive on-the-job training and promote professional development. As such, they will gradually learn to critically evaluate the technology content and adapt the available technology to their particular needs.

- Build and maintain an online forum to support communities of practice for people who share the same interest. For example, the Little Elit (http://littleelit.com/) provides a platform for librarians in the United States to share their viewpoints, experiences and presentations on the topic of young children, new media, and libraries. Additionally, Facebook provides a free online platform for people to exchange their opinions, discuss solutions to their problems and share their experiences.

References

1 Morgan, A., & Siraj-Blatchford, J. (2013). *Using ICT in the Early Years: Parents and Practitioners in Partnership. (2nd ed.)* London: Practical Pre-School Books.

2 Wood, E., & Attfield, J. (2005). *Play, Learning and the Early Childhood Curriculum (2nd ed.).* London: Paul Chapman Publishing.

3 Tamburrini, J. (1982). Some educational implications of Piaget's Theory. In S. Modgil, & C. Modgil (Eds.), *Jean Piaget: Consensus and Controversy* (pp. 309–325). New York: Praeger.

4 Siraj-Blatchford, J., and Siraj-Blatchford, I. (2002) *More than Computers: ICT in the Early Years, Early Education/ British Association for Early Childhood Education*

5 National Association for the Education of Young Children (NAEYC) (2012) *Technology and Interactive Media as Tools in Early Childhood Programs Serving Children from Birth through Age 8*, Accessed at: http://www.naeyc.org/content/technology-and-young-children

6 Siraj-Blatchford, I. (2007). Creativity, communication and collaboration: The identification of pedagogic progression in sustained shared thinking. *Asia-Pacific Journal of Research in Early Childhood Education*, 1(2), 3–23.

7 Guernsey, L. (2012). *Screen Time: How Electronic Media – From Baby Videos to Educational Software – Affects Your Young Child.* New York: Basic Books.

Choosing the right resources

A growing consensus has emerged regarding the most appropriate forms that ICT education should take in early childhood. Eight general principles have been identified for determining the effectiveness of ICT applications, or uses of ICT in the early years, to help caregivers (e.g. parents, pre-school teachers and librarians) provide the best possible experiences (Siraj-Blatchford and Siraj-Blatchford, 2006)[1]. They are:

- Ensure an educational purpose.

- Encourage child collaboration.

- Integrate ICT with other activities away from the screen.

- Support the child's play.

- Ensure that the child is in control.

- Choose applications that are intuitively understandable.

- Avoid applications that portray violence or stereotyping.

- Be aware of the health and safety issues, and

- Support parent – professional partnership.

Here are some tips for consideration when choosing the 'right' resources to use with children:

App reviews: Considering the 100,000s of educational Apps currently available on the Apple and Google online App stores, it can often be a minefield for parents to choose the right App for their child. When reading the reviews, caregivers need to be cautious as these review comments can be biased. Fortunately, there are several websites providing guidance for parents/carers and offering expert's and parents' reviews of best Apps and other technologies.

- Common Sense Media (https://www.commonsensemedia.org/app-reviews): Provides unbiased ratings conducted by expert reviewers and not influenced by the creators of specific Apps or individual funders. On the website, parents can choose a resource according to their child's age (2-17); entertainment type (e.g. games, websites, Apps); device (e.g. iPad, Android, Kindle Fire); price; genre (e.g. action game, puzzle game, role playing, word game); subject (e.g. Language, Maths, Science); skill (e.g. emotional development, creativity, reasoning) or learner rating. The website also allows parents to choose according to children's topic preferences (e.g. dinosaurs, princesses, bugs) and parents' own recommendations.

- TEEM (http://teemeducation.org.uk/early-years): Offering teachers and classroom practitioners information (e.g. evaluations, case studies and reviews) on digital resources to help them find and use the best technology to assist their teaching.

- Children's Technology Review (http://childrenstech.com/): Providing helpful tips and reviews of digital products that parents can choose from. Parents can select Apps according to children's ages, school subjects and platforms (e.g. Kindle, iPad and Android). Parents can add their comments to the expert reviews, which are verified by several other external organisations, including the KAPi Awards and the BolognaRagazzi Digital Award.

- App Playground (http://Appsplayground.com): Listing best Apps according to age, basic categories (playful/educational) and device.

- Moms with Apps (https://knowwhatsinside.com/discover): Offering a wide range of parental reviews of specific Apps, categorised according to children's age (0-2) and a range of subjects (e.g. art, colours, animals or shapes).

- Little Elite (http://littleelit.com/): A grass-roots professional learning network that recommends Apps and suggests practices to incorporate new media (e.g. Apps) into library collections, services and programmes for families with young children.

- School Library Journal (http://www.slj.com/category/technology/Apps-tech/): Providing reviews on selected Apps, recommending top Apps and offering information regarding children's usage of ICT.

- The Horn Book (http://www.hbook.com/category/choosing-books/app-review-of-the-week/): Offering weekly reviews of new Apps under discussion.

Usability: Caregivers need to consider whether the App is easy to navigate and whether the interface is user-friendly in children's terms. Remember that the intention here is not for children to master their ICT skills but to support their learning. Difficulties in the usage of an App can cause frustration for the children and deter them from learning. It is essential to create a positive learning environment for enhancing children's learning outputs. For example, the Our Story™ App is easy to use and uses large iconic buttons that help eliminate language barriers.

Flexibility: A good App should afford you to adjust the level of complexity of a game to the ability of your intended children. Some Apps even allow you to personalise the content. For example, Bitsboard – Memory Cards™ offers a range of choices, including: the content of the memory cards, the number of memory cards, the number of players, and different matching options (e.g. image to image, text to text, image to audio and image to text).

Payment: The price of Apps varies and it normally shows at App Store and Google Play Store. Some paid Apps provide a free lite version (with limited functions/experiences) for trial, and there are also Apps that are completely free. When using free Apps, be wary of any inappropriate advertisement pop-ups for children.

References

1   Siraj-Blatchford, I., & Siraj-Blatchford, J. (2006). *A Curriculum Development Guide to ICT in Early Childhood Education*. Nottingham: Trentham Books with Early Education.

Apps mentioned in the book

Raising expectations and achievement

- Bee-Bot™
- Move the Turtle™
- Daisy the Dinosaur™
- Cargo Bot™
- ScratchJr™
- Hopscotch™
- Kodable™

- Get Water™
- Zoe makes a splash!™
- Green Rank – Save our Oceans™
- RecyClaire™
- Gimme Gimme™
- The Lorax™
- Green Up™

Peer-to-peer play

- Puppet Pals HD™
- Pic Collage™
- Popplet™
- Our Story™
- Finger Paint With Sounds™
- My PlayHome Stores™
- Toca Pet Doctor™
- Tizzy Veterinarian HD™
- Bitsboard – Memory Cards™
- Me Books™

Adult-child play

- My Story™
- StoryMaker™

Information and Communications

- Gro Garden™
- Gro Recycling™
- Toca Nature™

Conclusion

As we have shown, a wide range of programmable toys, educational programs and Apps can be used to support children's early learning and development, perhaps most significantly in terms of their literacy, verbal reflection and abstract thinking. This is not a new idea. Bowman et al.'s (2001, p.229)[1] highly influential US National Research Council research review, *Eager to Learn*, strongly endorsed the use of computers in early childhood fourteen years ago:

> *Computers help even young children think about thinking, as early proponents suggested (Papert, 1980)[2]. In one study, preschoolers who used computers scored higher on measures of metacognition (Fletcher-Flinn & Suddendorf, 1996)[3]. They were more able to keep in mind a number of different mental states simultaneously and had more sophisticated theories of mind than those who did not use computers.*

ICTs have also been found to provide significant support to educators in terms of their pedagogic knowledge (Siraj-Blatchford & Parmar, 2011)[4]. US research has provided direct evidence of the effectiveness of applying ICT in the home. For example, McCarrick et al. (2007)[5] interviewed 136 parents of Head Start children who owned a computer to identify the frequency and type of involvement that they had with their children while at the computer. They found that young children performed better on measures of cognitive competence (verbal, quantitative, general cognitive, and memory) and school readiness when their parents were actively involved with their home computer use:

> *[...] the benefits of parental involvement were not observed among children whose parents were passively involved (e.g., watched the child use the computer).*

Although children can learn collaboratively and independently, and they often do so very well, they should not be left alone to use ICT. Caregivers (e.g. parents, pre-school teachers and librarians) are responsible for ensuring that children respond positively to the digital tools, adjust the complexity level of the activity to children's abilities, and effectively extend children's discussion around their digital play. Furthermore, the existence of digital tools is not to replace, but to support the pedagogical role of caregivers in terms of enhancing child learning and development. For example, in the research of Falloon and Khoo (2014)[6], Puppet Pals HD™ were used to support the recounting of stories; Pic Collage™ for summarising learning from a unit of celebrations; Popplet™ for story plan development. Therefore, it is critical how pre-school teachers integrate Apps into their school curricula, parents use Apps in the home learning environment, and librarians incorporate Apps in the programmes for young children.

Personalising books can be a great way to engage young children more deeply in a story and show them the potential rewards of reading. Emerging research shows that books which are personalised encourage children to speak more about the book they read (Kucirkova et al., 2014)[7]. However, the content of children's talk is predominantly self-centred, which means that they focus more on their own feelings rather than those of others or of other story characters. It is therefore important that personalised books are used always in conjunction with

non-personalised stories which broaden children's horizons. By creating their own story contents, children can record their own stories, which reflect their view of the real world and learn about writing, sequencing and other emergent literacy skills. This is very important as they develop their confidence in reading and writing. In addition, various language variants of the same book can help families learn new languages, especially linguistic minority families learning a national language.

In order to reap the benefits of social interaction, a story App needs to strike a judicious balance between providing motivation and support, and inviting young children to be creators, not just consumers of the digital content. Personalisation can involve and empower children, yet complicated Apps with too many 'bells and whistles' simply overwhelm them. Not many App designers have quite accomplished this balance yet. Caregivers therefore need to look for Apps that support balanced experiences for young children.

Technological development continues to move forward at an ever-increasing pace, and this has profound implications for society. The pace of change in modern societies is particularly challenging for the school curriculum, which must respond

Outstanding Practice (OFSTED, 2013)[8]

Achieving Outstanding practice in ICT Education at the Foundation level involves seven key areas of curriculum development identified by OFSTED (2013), each of these have been addressed throughout this text:

- Having high expectations of children and presenting positive role models

- Providing stimulating, inspirational, and highly motivating practical activities

- Showing practice that is innovative and worthy of dissemination to other providers

- Engaging and involving parents, and supporting the child's home learning environment

- Providing focussed documentation and clear bases for assessments

- Providing clear and relevant preparation for schooling

- Providing safety and risk management.

In addition, ICT and 'computational thinking' practices have been identified that will support wider curriculum objectives in countering inequality, underachievement and social justice.

(however indirectly) to these economic and cultural changes. The three- and four-year-olds of today will complete their high school education in 2028 and 2029, and, given the exponential rate of technological development and advance that we are already experiencing, we can be sure that the economic and cultural realities at that time will be quite different to those experienced today. It is now widely recognised that technology must broaden and balance the curriculum alongside literature, science and music as a major cultural form in its own right.

References

1   Bowman, B.T., M.S. Donovan, & M.S. Burns (Eds.) (2001). *Eager to Learn: Educating Our Preschoolers*. Washington, DC: National Academy Press.

2   Papert, S. (1980). Mindstorms: *Children, Computers, and Powerful Ideas*. New York: Basic Books.

3   Fletcher-Flinn, C., & Suddendorf, T. (1996). Do computers affect the mind? *Journal of Educational Computing Research*, 15(2), 97–112.

4   Siraj-Blatchford, J., & Parmar, N. (2011). Knowledge learning processes and ICT in early childhood education. *He Kupu*, 2(5), 45–60.

5   McCarrick, K., Lia, X., Fisha, A., Holtropa, T., Bhavnagrib, N.P., Stantona, B., Brumittc, G.A., Butlera, S., & Partridged, T. (2007). Parental involvement in young children's computer use and cognitive development. *NHSA Dialog: A Research-to-Practice Journal for the Early Childhood Field*, 10(2), 67–82.

6   Falloon, G., & Khoo, E. (2014). Exploring young students' talk in iPad-supported collaborative learning environments. *Computers & Education*, 77, 13–28.

7   Kucirkova, N., Messer, D., & Sheehy, K. (2014). The effects of personalisation on young children's spontaneous speech during shared book reading. *Journal of Pragmatics*, 71, 45–55.

8   Office for Standards in Education, Children's Services and Skills (OFSTED) (2013) *Evaluation schedule for inspections of registered early years provision: Guidance and grade descriptors for inspecting registered early years provision* from 4 November 2013.

Glossary

3G: Short form of third generation, a mobile communications standard that allows mobile phones, computers, and other portable electronic devices to access the Internet wirelessly.

4G: Short for fourth generation, a mobile communications standard intended to replace 3G, allowing wireless Internet access at a much higher speed.

Android: An increasingly popular operating system for smartphones.

Apps: An 'application' is a software program. While the shortened term 'app' was used exclusively in the past in the context of smart phones and tablets it is increasingly being applied in the context of desktop and laptop computer programs.

Blog: Short for "Web Log," this term refers to a list of journal entries posted on a Web page.

Cyberbulling: Cyberbullying takes place over cyberspace. This includes both Internet and cell phone communication. Like physical bullying, cyberbullying is aimed at younger people, such as children and teenagers. It may involve harassing, threatening, embarrassing, or humiliating young people online.

Desktop computer: A computer that is designed to stay in a single location. Unlike laptops and other portable devices, desktop computers cannot be powered from an internal battery and therefore must remain connected to a wall outlet.

Download: The act of retrieving software, files, or information using an Internet connection. This is the area in which the speed difference between dial-up and high-speed Internet service is the most pronounced. Files that take hours to download using a dial-up connection can take just minutes or seconds using a high-speed connection.

Filter: Software that gives you the ability to control content displayed, block websites and set up passwords to protect children/adults from pornography, chat sites etc.

Facebook: A social networking website.

Video Game console: A device that outputs a video signal or visual image to display a video game.

Global Positioning System (GPS): A satellite-based navigation system that provides location and time information in all weather conditions, anywhere on or near the earth where there is an unobstructed line of sight to four or more GPS satellites.

Handheld device (a.k.a. mobile device): A small computing device, typically small enough to be handheld, having a display screen with touch input and/or a miniature keyboard and weighing less than 2 pounds (0.91 kg). Samsung, Sony, HTC, LG, Motorola Mobility and Apple are just a few examples of the many manufacturers that produce these types of devices.

Information Communications and Technology (ICT): Technologies that provide access to information through telecommunications. It is similar to Information Technology (IT), but focuses primarily on communication technologies. This includes the Internet, wireless networks, cell phones, and other communication mediums.

Internet: A worldwide association of interconnected networks of connected computers. This network provides for the transfer of files, remote login, electronic mail, news, search and other services.

Interactive Whiteboard (IW): A large wall or board mounted display which is connected to a computer and projector that allows user interaction via a pen or finger.

iOS: A mobile operating system developed by Apple. It was originally named the iPhone OS, but was renamed to the iOS in June, 2009. The iOS currently runs on the iPhone, iPod touch, and iPad.

iPhone: A smartphone developed by Apple.

iPod: A portable music player developed by Apple.

iPad: A tablet computer developed by Apple.

Kindle: A portable e-reader developed by Amazon.com. It allows you to download and read digital books, newspapers, magazines, and other electronic publications. The Kindle also includes a built-in speaker and headphone jack for listening to audiobooks or background music.

Laptop: A small, portable computer, also referred to as a notebook.

Leapster: The Leapster Learning Game System is an educational handheld game console aimed at 4 to 10 year olds (pre-school to fourth grade), made by LeapFrog Enterprises. Its games teach the alphabet, phonics, basic math (addition, subtraction, multiplication, division), and art and animal facts to players.

LeapTV: A TV connected video game console that uses motion control, produced by LeapFrog.

Monitor: A monitor displays the computer's user interface and open programs, allowing the user to interact with the computer, typically using the keyboard and mouse.

Operating System (OS): The main software program that runs the computer. Popular operating systems (OS) include Windows, Mac OS, Android, LINUX and UNIX.

Personal Computer (PC): A typical PC includes a system unit, monitor, keyboard, and mouse. Most PCs today also have a network or Internet connection, as well as ports for connecting peripheral devices, such as digital cameras, printers, scanners, speakers, external hard drives, and other components.

Projector: A device that projects an image onto a screen or other surface.

Scanner: A device for capturing a digital image of a drawing or picture.

Smartphone: All mobile telephones are computerised but 'smartphones' are mobile telephones with wireless (radio) internet access, and the capability of running Apps (see above).

Software: Computer programmes (often contrasted with 'hardware' – the physical equipment of a computer system and/or 'liveware' – the human user/operators of computer systems, who are sometimes considered to merely complement the hardware and software!)

Tablet: A display that can detect the presence and location of a touch of a finger within the display area.

YouTube: A video sharing service that allows users to watch videos posted by other users and upload videos of their own, like Vimeo.

Video Graphics Array (VGA): The standard monitor or display interface used in most PCs. If a monitor is VGA-compatible, it should work with most new computers.

Xbox: A very popular video game console from Microsoft.

Website: Pages posted on the internet. These pages are accessed using an URL (Uniform Resource Identifier) and may be maintained by an ISP (Internet Service Provider) or other individual or institution with the appropriate 'server'.

WiFi: A technology that allows a computer, smartphone or peripheral device to connect to other devices and/or the internet wirelessly (using radio waves). For most practical purposes the term WiFi can also be used synonymously with the term 'wireless local area network' (WLAN).

Wii: A popular video game console from Nintendo.

Acknowledgements

Photo credits

Every effort has been made to locate copyright owners of the images used in this book. Permission to use photographic images was given by the individuals and institutions listed below. Omissions brought to our attention will be corrected. For permission to reproduce these images please contact the owners.

Cover images:

Main image and middle left: photos taken by Hui-Yun Sung © MA Education Ltd

Middle centre: © iStockphoto.com/diego_cervo

Middle right: photo taken by Ben Suri © MA Education Ltd.

Back cover (left-right): © iStockphoto.com/naumoid, © iStockphoto.com/vladacanon.

Inners:

Page 2 © iStockphoto.com/kwanisik

Page 3 © iStockphoto.com/Imagesbybarbara

Page 4 © iStockphoto.com/Ridvan Celik

Page 5 © iStockphoto.com/Peter Booth

Page 6 photo taken by Lucie Carlier © MA Education Ltd

Page 7 © iStockphoto.com/kirill4mula

Page 11 © iStockphoto.com/vladacanon. Icons made by Freepix from www.flaticon.com

Page 12 © iStockphoto.com/Lise Gagne

Page 16 © iStockphoto.com/boggy22

Page 18 © iStockphoto.com/onebluelight

Page 20 © iStockphoto.com/michellegibson

Pages 23, 27, 32, 42 and 45 © iStockphoto.com/Susan Chiang

Page 25, 37 © iStockphoto.com/SolStock

Page 26 © iStockphoto.com/michellegibson

Page 28 © iStockphoto.com/Courtney Keating

Pages 29 and 43 © iStockphoto.com/lostinbids

Page 30 © iStockphoto.com/naumoid

Page 31 © iStockphoto.com/mmpile

Page 33 © iStockphoto.com/RyanKing999

Page 35 © iStockphoto.com/Dean Mitchell

Page 38 © iStockphoto.com/Dragonvanish

Page 40 © iStockphoto.com/Yobro10

Page 43 © iStockphoto.com/diego_cervo